高等院校经济管理类信息技术实验系列教材

信息系统导论实验教程

李艳红　主　编

杜梅先　副主编

上海财经大学出版社

图书在版编目(CIP)数据

信息系统导论实验教程/李艳红主编.—上海：上海财经大学出版社，2018.1
（高等院校经济管理类信息技术实验系列教材）
ISBN 978-7-5642-2894-1/F•2894

Ⅰ.①信… Ⅱ.①李… Ⅲ.①信息系统-实验-高等学校-教材 Ⅳ.①G202-33

中国版本图书馆 CIP 数据核字(2017)第 304314 号

□ 责任编辑　吴晓群
□ 封面设计　张克瑶

XINXI XITONG DAOLUN SHIYAN JIAOCHENG
信 息 系 统 导 论 实 验 教 程

李艳红　主　编
杜梅先　副主编

上海财经大学出版社出版发行
（上海市中山北一路369号　邮编 200083）
网　　址：http://www.sufep.com
电子邮箱：webmaster @ sufep.com
全国新华书店经销
上海叶大印务发展有限公司印刷装订
2018年1月第1版　2018年1月第1次印刷

787mm×1092mm　1/16　7.5印张　192千字
印数：0 001—2 000　　定价：39.00元

高等院校经济管理类信息技术实验系列教材

编委会

主　编　刘兰娟

副主编　韩冬梅　韩景侗　李艳红

编委会　（按姓氏笔画排序）

王炳雪	邓祖新	王淞昕	冯佳昕	田　博
刘兰娟	竹宇光	陈元忠	陈　岗	芮廷先
邵志芳	李欣苗	吴继兰	李艳红	杜梅先
张　勇	张　娥	张雪凤	劳帼龄	郑大庆
郝晓玲	赵龙强	曹　风	崔丽丽	黄海量
曾庆丰	韩冬梅	韩松乔	谢美萍	韩景侗
熊珺杰				

总 序

科技在飞速发展,社会在不断进步,当代大学生若要适应市场经济对人才的需求,除了要有深厚的理论基础,更需要具有实践能力,因此,大学的实验教学和实践体系设计越发重要,成为在校生学习和受教育过程的重要组成部分。

高等学校IT人才的创新和实践能力与社会岗位需求之间存在一定差距,很重要的一个原因是高校实验课程的设计与企业需求联系不够紧密,实验课程设置中整体思想贯穿不够。所以,为了加快经济管理类高校IT类实验课程的建设步伐,需要在新一轮课程体系改革中,围绕"能力分解、阶梯推进"的课程实验改革思路,基于阶段项目训练的课程体系建设规划,同时结合IT相关专业的特点,在遵循现有课程体系的前提下,对专业课程的实验环节进行重组、整合和系统性规划,将IT行业的职业化场景真正引入课程体系和教学的全过程。

根据实验教学规律,我们将实验教学分为基础认知型(软件实验和硬件实验)、应用设计型、综合创新型(包括课程性综合实验、专业性综合实验、学科性综合实验)三个层次。分层次安排实验项目和内容,实现实验教学的系统优化。通过基础认知型实验设计,对学生进行基本实验技能、实验原理、实验方法的训练,巩固和应用理论知识;通过应用设计型实验设计,让学生能够运用基础实验内容,通过比较、抽象、概括、归纳等积极思维活动进行课程设计;通过综合创新型实验设计,运用多门课程的实验内容和实验结果,提出实现综合设计实验的总体方案,充分发挥学生的积极性、主动性和创造性,促进知识向能力转化。通过以上三个层次的实验设计规划,形成彼此关联、相互配合的系统化、层次化的实验课程体系。在这一过程中强调在课程群中统一实验目标、集中规划,在各门课程认知实验的基础上,强调专业知识的集成和学科综合。与此同时,利用"案例与任务驱动"的教学模式,启发学生在课程群环境中通过演练式学习主动分析和研究企业仿真环境,发现问题,创新思维,培养大学生的创造性思维。

本系列实验教材具有一定的实践意义:(1)形成了分阶段、渐进式学习模式,课程体系在原有的单一性、演示型、验证性课程实验的基础上设计了设计型、综合性实验,以及开放性、创新型实验,引导学生由浅入深,从知识理解到知识运用,再从知识运用到自主创新。(2)设计了以知识贯穿和课程融合为主导的集成实验内容,实现了十几门课程、基于两个案例的实验课程集成,弥补了课程之间的知识断点,实现了各课程之间的知识融合,促使学生从科目分科学习到知识融会贯通,从各门课程的知识积累向所有知识的综合运用能力转化。

本系列实验教材分专业和公共两个系列:专业系列包括综合设计实验、数据库、系统分析与设计、管理信息系统等实验教材;公共系列包括管理会计、经济管理中的计算机应用、ERP综合实验等实验教材。本系列实验教材既适合作为高等学校信息管理与信息系统专业和经济管理类的IT专业本科生学习及实践的配套指导教材,也可以作为非计算机专业学生教学实践课程的专用教材。

希望通过本系列实验教材的共享和传播,能促进上海财经大学IT专业实验教学的深入开展,助力于全国财经类院校经管类IT专业实验教学的改革探索,继而推动全国高等院校实验教学的创新发展。

刘兰娟
上海财经大学信息管理与工程学院
2018年1月

前 言

"信息系统导论"课程,又名"管理信息系统"课程,是信息管理与信息系统、电子商务专业的专业核心课或专业方向课,在专业课体系中是重点,它注重理论联系实际、注重实验。在"管理信息系统"课程实验教学中,通过渐进、动态的实验教学环节改变传统管理信息系统教学单一接受性、强迫性的教学特征,根据专业特点,按照教学规律和教学内容,将管理信息系统实践教学划分层次,合理地组成体系,形成既相对独立、又相互联系的实践性能力培养体系,使学生在教师的指导和参与下,能够在有限的时间内,更好地将课堂知识与实际应用相结合,增强学生独立思考的能力,提高学生的综合素质和实际动手能力。本实验教材作为"信息系统导论"课程的实验指导,适应管理信息系统类课程实验教学的需求,作为该课程的有力支撑,促进该课程实验质量的提升,理论联系实践,提高学生的动手能力和解决实际问题的能力。

本实验教材在实验安排上以管理信息系统的感性认识和学习为主;既有独立试验,又有集成实验,与其他课程实验相呼应和衔接;既有英文实验、又有中文实验,适合不同教学目的和对象的需要;有实验目的、实验原理、实验环境、实验步骤等内容,指导细致;同时配备实验报告。本实验教材的实验设计强调内容上的实践性,使学生通过实践环节亲身体会信息系统的方方面面,增强其动手能力和解决实际问题的能力,帮助其巩固和加深课堂教学内容,提高其实际工作能力,培养科学作风,为其学习后续课程和从事实践技术工作奠定基础。

本实验教材具有以下特色:

(1)与特定教材相结合,实验步骤具体、指导深入。

(2)专门针对财经类院校信息管理类专业本科生"管理信息系统"课程实验环节的需要而编写。

(3)中英文结合,适合双语课程的需要。

(4)配备实验报告。

本实验讲义已试用3个学年,在试用过程中进行了不断的补充和改进,教学效果显著。编者在该课程的教学过程中已经总结摸索出一套可行且有效的实验教法,既获得了学生的一致好评,也更好地提高了学生的实践动手能力。目前,市场上的同类教材较多,但没有与当前的经典流行教材——斯蒂芬·哈格的《信息时代的管理信息系统》相配套的教材,且现在的"管理信息系统"课程大多是双语课程,要求相关资料,包括实验必须采用英语。本实验教材可供与时俱进、使用上述经典流行教材的兄弟院校选用。

编 者

2018年1月

实验教学提示

实验教学大纲

课程名称	信息系统导论/管理信息系统	课程性质	学科共同课
课程学时	64	实验学时	6
面向专业	信息管理与信息系统、电子商务、计算机科学		
实验室	多媒体教室、自由选择		
预修课程	程序设计基础、数据结构、面向对象的程序设计		

一、本实验课程的教学目的和任务

在"管理信息系统"实验教学中,通过渐进、动态的实验教学环节改变传统管理信息系统教学单一接受性、强迫性的教学特征,根据专业特点,按照教学规律和教学内容,将管理信息系统实践教学划分层次,合理地组成体系,形成既相对独立、又相互联系的实践性能力培养体系,使学生在教师的指导和参与下,能够在有限的时间内,更好地将课堂知识和实际应用相结合,增强学生独立思考的能力,提高学生的综合素质和实际动手能力。

二、本实验课程的基本要求

本实验课程的基本要求是对学生实验技能、创新能力、科研能力及解决实际问题方面的锻炼。管理信息系统实验是学习"管理信息系统"课程的一个重要环节。本实验开设对象为"管理信息系统"课程的学习者,实验为必修内容。

实验安排上以管理信息系统的感性认识和学习为主。实验设计强调内容上的实践性,使学生通过实践环节亲身体会信息系统的方方面面,增强其动手能力和解决实际问题的能力,帮助其巩固和加深课堂教学内容,提高其实际工作能力,培养科学作风,为其学习后续课程和从事实践技术工作奠定基础。

三、本实验课程与其他课程的关系

在教学计划安排上,通常是在第二学年讲授"管理信息系统"这门课程时,辅之本实验课程,这样有助于巩固、深化和拓展之前讲授的相关课程,如数据结构、程序设计基础和面向对象的程序设计,并为后续的专业核心课程,如数据库、信息系统分析和设计等,打下良好的铺垫和基础。本实验课程不仅能起到承上启下的作用,还会带给学生一个对管理信息系统的完整认识和体验。

独立实验部分

一、实验课程理论教学内容安排

计划占用教学计划内 64 课时中的 6 课时完成实验课程理论教学内容。

1	教学内容	Computer Hardware and Software	时数	2
2	教学内容	Microsoft Access Introduction	时数	1
3	教学内容	Operating DSS Systems	时数	2
4	教学内容	E-Commerce Business Models	时数	1

二、实验课程教学内容安排

要求占用学生课下约 8 课时的时间完成实验环节的任务。

	实验项目	Identifying Hardware and Software	时数	项目性质			
1	实验内容及要求	内容:在实验理论教学(熟悉软硬件)的基础上,学生能够根据自己的需要自行配置电脑。 要求: 　(1)明确自身需求,可选角色有研究生、设计师、游戏玩家。 　(2)记录电脑配置结果,提交实验报告。	2	验证	综合	设计	其他
	实验项目	Implementing a Database with Microsoft Access	时数	项目性质			
2	实验内容及要求	内容:熟悉一个小型的数据库产品(如 Microsoft Access),熟悉其中的库表、数据字典、查询功能、窗体生成功能和报表生成功能。使学生了解数据库的特点,通过窗体和报表的生成体会程序的自动编写和系统生成。 要求: 　(1)根据实验指南进行操作。 　(2)记录实验结果,填写实验报告。	3	验证	综合	设计	其他
	实验项目	Operating DSS Systems	时数	项目性质			
3	实验内容及要求	内容：基于演示系统库,包括业务处理系统、管理信息系统、决策支持系统、协作系统、地理信息系统等。学生模拟系统用户,按照系统设定的业务流程,完成相应的业务,了解如何在管理信息系统中实现企业运作、企业管理。 要求: 　(1)学生在演示系统库中至少挑选一种类型的系统(目前固定为 DSS)进行体验并分析评价。 　(2)填写实验报告。	2	验证	综合	设计	其他

续表

	实验项目	E-Commerce Business Models	时数	项目性质			
				验证	综合	设计	其他
4	实验内容及要求	内容：模拟网上交易操作过程，了解企业各项业务活动的数据流程和相关处理过程。同时，强调客户关系管理的重要性，让学生亲自观察客户关系管理系统的功能和特点，并评价设计客户关系管理方法。 要求： 　　(1)B2B、B2C、C2C 网上交易（三选一）模拟实验。 　　(2)填写实验报告。	1				

集成实验部分

一、实验课程理论教学内容安排

计划占用教学计划内 64 课时中的 6 课时完成实验课程理论教学内容。

1	教学内容	Ch.3 Databases and Data Warehouses Relational Database Models Relational Database Design Microsoft Access	时数	2
2	教学内容	Ch.4 Decision Support and Artificial Intelligence Concepts of Decision Support System Examples of DSS Components of a DSS	时数	2
3	教学内容	Ch.5 Electronic Commerce E-Commerce Business Models B2C E-Commerce Understand Your Business, Products, Services, and Customers by B2C and B2B	时数	1
4	教学内容	Ch.6 Systems Development Systems Development Life Cycle： 　Planning, Analysis, Design, Development, Testing, Implementation, Maintenance	时数	1

二、实验课程教学内容安排

要求占用学生课下约 8 课时的时间完成实验环节的任务。

1	实验项目	集成实验1:保证输入数据的正确性	时数	项目性质			
	实验内容及要求	(1)在 Microsoft Access 数据库中建立网上商城"产品类别表"。 要求: ①表中含有三列,分别是类别 ID、类别名称、典型图片; ②类别 ID 构成是 1 位数字加下划线加三个字母形式,如"1_ABC"; ③类别名称只限于"手机导航仪、电脑设备、办公设备、数码产品、电视家庭影音、厨卫器具"六种; ④图片是对象连接与嵌入类型。 (2)将"网上商城系统数据库"中的数据表 tb_class 导入 ACCESS 数据库,表名不变。 (3)填写实验报告。	2	验证	综合	设计	其他
2	实验项目	集成实验2:网上商城的销售决策分析	时数	项目性质			
	实验内容及要求	(1)利用 Microsoft Office,查询汇总销售数据,并预测未来的销售情况。 采用合适的方法,查询"网上商城系统数据库数据.xls"文件中 2010 年 1 月到 2011 年 10 月的销售数据,将这些数据按照月份进行汇总,并利用汇总结果,预测未来一个月——2011 年 11 月的销售情况。 (2)填写实验报告。	2	验证	综合	设计	其他
3	实验项目	集成实验3:网上商城的前后台功能体验	时数	项目性质			
	实验内容及要求	(1)前台操作 连接网上商城(http://202.121.143.200:801)。 ①注册一个用户; ②完成一个商品的购买流程,总结购买流程; ③进行虚拟充值。 (2)后台操作 ①添加一个新的管理员; ②添加 2 件商品。 (3)结合知名网站亚马逊,分析该网站的优缺点,给出提升其功能的建议。 (4)填写实验报告。	3	验证	综合	设计	其他
4	实验项目	集成实验4:走近系统分析设计文档	时数	项目性质			
	实验内容及要求	(1)在相关文档阅读的基础上,回答以下问题: ①系统开发生命周期法(SDLC 法)的文档有什么特点和作用? ②系统分析文档如何转化为系统设计文档? ③探讨系统分析与设计对系统实现的影响。 ④评价该网上商城文档的优劣之处,并指出需要提高的地方。 (2)填写实验报告。	1	验证	综合	设计	其他

三、实验报告及考核要求（包括对实验报告的考核要求和对该实验课程的考核要求）

实验必须循序渐进地进行，不能急躁冒进。很多实验内容需要掌握的基础知识较多，所以实验准备尤其需要下功夫，只有这样才能理清实验的目的、要求，列出实验的步骤，对可能出现的问题做好充分的准备。

实验前必须明确实验目的，理解实验原理；了解实验环境；了解实验方法，拟订实验的操作步骤。实验过程中需认真观察实验现象，详细记录实验结果。实验后通过对实验记录的整理，从理论上加以分析归纳，以加深对所学理论知识的理解，不断总结、积累经验，从而提高动手能力。

对实验报告的要求：(1) 按时参加实验；(2) 提交实验报告。

实验报告的考核分为优、良、中、及格和不及格。

实验课程的成绩记入课程平时成绩，占总成绩的 10%。

四、选用教材及参考书

指定教材：

Stephen Haag, Maeve Cummings, *Management Information Systems for the Information Age* (9th Edition)，(《信息时代的管理信息系统》，英文版·原书第 9 版)，机械工业出版社 2017 年版。

参考书目：

（美）肯尼思·劳东(Kenneth C. Laudon)，简·劳东(Jane P. Laudon)著，劳帼龄译：《管理信息系统》(第 13 版)，中国人民大学出版社 2016 年版。

（美）斯蒂芬·哈格(Stephen Haag)，梅芙·卡明斯(Maeve Cummings)著，颜志军等译：《信息时代的管理信息系统》(原书第 9 版)，机械工业出版社 2016 年版。

其他参考材料：本课程的实验指导书。

目 录

总序 ……………………………………………………………………………………… 1

前言 ……………………………………………………………………………………… 1

实验教学提示 …………………………………………………………………………… 1

第一部分 独立实验

1 Independent Experiment Guidance …………………………………………… 1

Independent Experiment Guidance 1：Introduction to Hardware and Software ………… 1

Independent Experiment Guidance 2：Implementing a Database With Microsoft Access
……………………………………………………………………………………… 7

Independent Experiment Guidance 3：Operating DSS Systems ………………………… 29

Independent Experiment Guidance 4：E-Commerce Business Models ………………… 41

2 Independent Experiment Report ………………………………………………… 43

Independent Experiment Report 1 ……………………………………………………… 43

Independent Experiment Report 2 ……………………………………………………… 46

Independent Experiment Report 3 ……………………………………………………… 49

Independent Experiment Report 4 ……………………………………………………… 52

第二部分　集成实验

1　集成实验指导 ··· 57
集成实验指导 1：保证输入数据的正确性 ···························· 57
集成实验指导 2：网上商城的销售决策分析 ························· 70
集成实验指导 3：网上商城的前后台功能体验 ····················· 83
集成实验指导 4：走近系统分析设计文档 ···························· 84

2　集成实验报告 ··· 90
集成实验报告 1 ··· 90
集成实验报告 2 ··· 93
集成实验报告 3 ··· 96
集成实验报告 4 ··· 99

参考文献 ·· 102

第一部分　独立实验

1 Independent Experiment Guidance

Independent Experiment Guidance 1:
Introduction to Hardware and Software

As the following, let's introduce software and hardware.

● **Software** — set of instructions that hardware executes to carry out a specific task for you, which includes the following two categories:

1. Application software — enable you to solve specific problems or perform specific tasks

2. System software — handle tasks specific to technology management and coordinate the interaction of all technology devices, which includes:

(1) **Operating system software** — control application software and manage hardware devices

(2) **Utility software** — provide additional functionality to your operating system, such as Anti-virus, Screen saver etc.

● **Hardware** — physical devices that make up a computer (or computer system). There are six categories of hardware as follows:

1. Input device — use to enter information and commands. Common input devices are as follows:

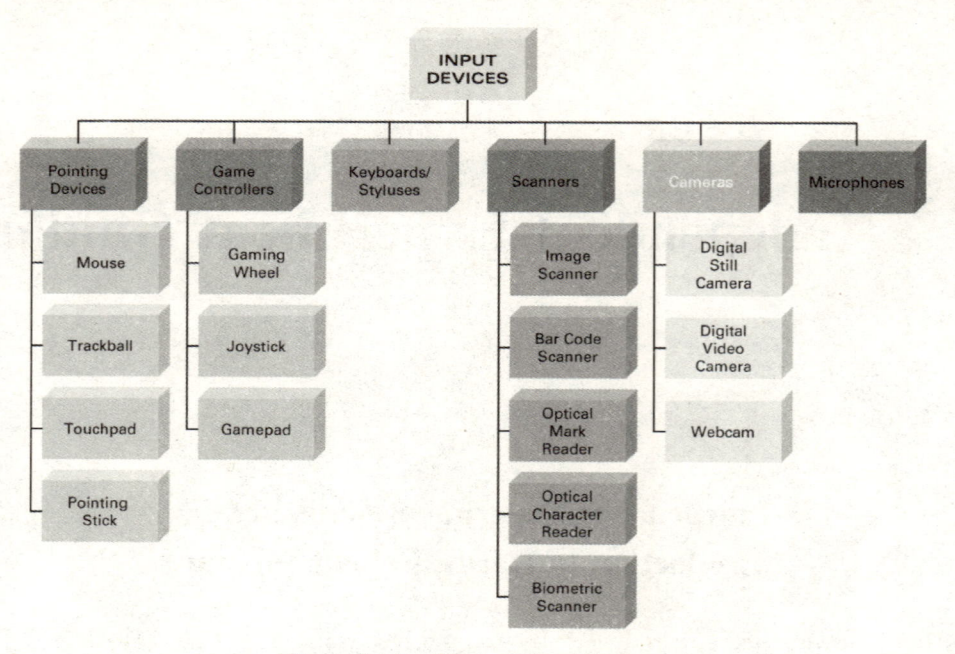

Figure 1.1.1　Common Input Devices

2. Output device — hear, see, or otherwise recognize the results of information-processing requests. Common output devices are as follows:

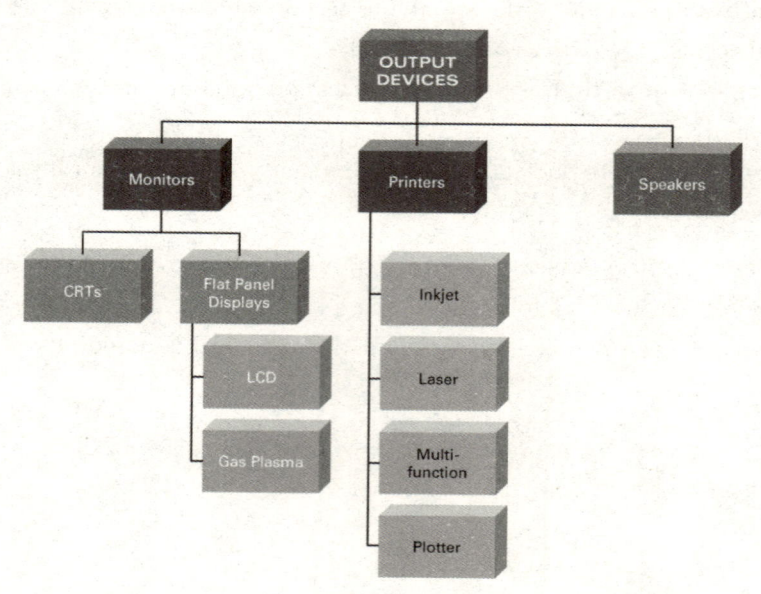

Figure 1.1.2　Common Output Devices

3. Storage device — store information for use at a later time. Common storage devices are as follows:

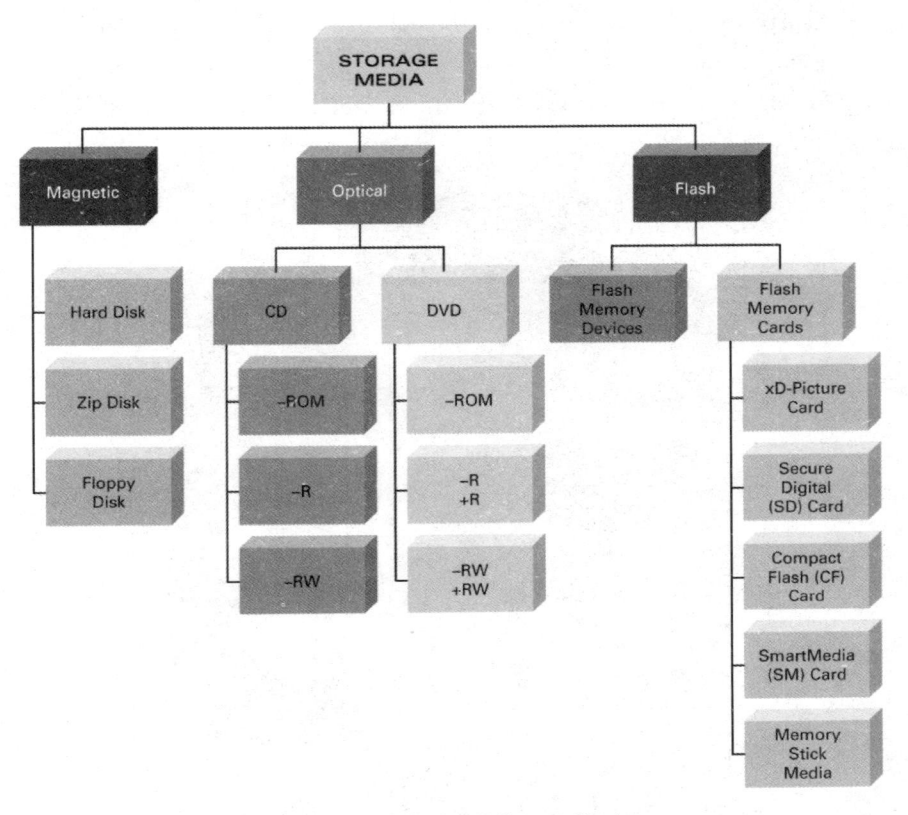

Figure 1.1.3 Common Storage Devices

4. Processing device, which includes:
(1) **CPU** — hardware that interprets and executes software and coordinates all hardware.
(2) **RAM** — temporary holding area for information and software.
CPU and RAM work together to form the brain of your computer.

The dominant manufacturers of CPU are such as Intel (Celeron, Pentium, Xeon) and AMD (Athlon, Opteron).

CPU speed measured in gigahertz(GHz).

5. Telecommunications device — send information to and receive it from another person or computer in a network. So you have to know network and modem.

Network — two or more computers connected so that they can communicate with each other and possibly share information, software, peripheral devices, and/or processing power.

Modem — connect a computer to a phone line to access another computer or network, to modulate outgoing signal from digital to analog form, and demodulate incoming signal from analog to digital form.

Communication software includes:
(1) **Connectivity software** — enable you to use your computer to "dial up" or connect to

another computer.

(2) **Web browser software** — enable you to surf the Web.

(3) **E-mail software** — enable you to electronically communicate with other people by sending and receiving e-mail.

6. Connecting device — let you connect peripherals to your computer, such as cables, ports, expansion boards etc. Common connectors and ports are as follows:

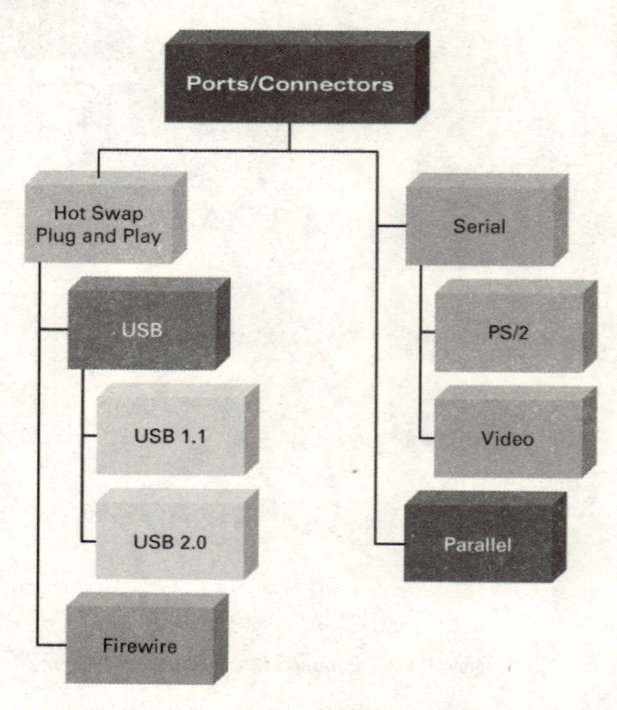

Figure 1.1.4 Common Connectors and Ports

Independent Experiment Guidance 2:
Implementing a Database with Microsoft Access

In this part, we will show how to implement a database with Microsoft Access.

- **Introduction**

The steps to creating a database are:

1. Define entity classes and primary keys
2. Define relationships among the entity classes
3. Define fields for each relation (file)
4. Use a data definition language to create the database, which is the focus of this Module

As the following, we've created the correct database structure, which is about Solomon Enterprise Database. Solomon Enterprise Database has the following tables(relations).

CONCRETE TYPE RELATION

Concrete Type	Type Description
1	Home foundation and walkways
2	Commercial foundation and walkways
3	Premier speckled (with smooth gravel aggregate)
4	Premier marble (with crushed marble aggregate)
5	Premier shell (with shell aggregate)

CUSTOMER RELATION

Customer Number	Customer Name	Customer Phone	Customer Primary Contact
1234	Smelding Homes	3333333333	Bill Johnson
2345	Home Builders Superior	3334444444	Marcus Connolly
3456	Mark Akey	3335555555	Mark Akey
4567	Triple A Homes	3336666666	Janielle Smith
5678	Sheryl Williamson	3337777777	Sheryl Williamson
6789	Home Makers	3338888888	John Yu

EMPLOYEE RELATION

Employee ID	Employee Last Name	Employee First Name	Date of Hire
123456789	Johnson	Emilio	2/1/1985
435296657	Evaraz	Antonio	3/3/1992
78934444	Robertson	John	6/1/1999
984568756	Smithson	Allison	4/1/1997

Figure 1.2.1　Concrete Type, Customer, and Employee Relations

SUPPLIER RELATION

Supplier ID	Supplier Name
412	Wesley Enterprises
444	Juniper Sand & Gravel
499	A&J Brothers
999	N/A

TRUCK RELATION

Truck Number	Truck Type	Date of Purchase
111	Ford	6/17/1999
222	Ford	12/24/2001
333	Chevy	1/1/2002

ORDER RELATION

Order Number	Order Date	Customer Number	Delivery Address	Concrete Type	Amount	Truck Number	Driver ID
100000	9/1/2004	1234	55 Smith Lane	1	8	111	123456789
100001	9/1/2004	3456	2122 E. Biscayne	1	3	222	785934444
100002	9/2/2004	1234	55 Smith Lane	5	6	222	435296657
100003	9/3/2004	4567	1333 Burr Ridge	2	4	333	435296657
100004	9/4/2004	4567	1333 Burr Ridge	2	8	222	785934444
100005	9/4/2004	5678	1222 Westminster	1	4	222	785934444
100006	9/5/2004	1234	222 East Hampton	1	4	111	123456789
100007	9/6/2004	2345	9 W. Palm Beach	2	5	333	785934444
100008	9/6/2004	6789	4532 Lane Circle	1	8	222	785934444
100009	9/7/2004	1234	987 Furlong	3	8	111	123456789
100010	9/9/2004	6789	4532 Lane Circle	2	7	222	435296657
100011	9/9/2004	4567	3500 Tomahawk	5	6	222	785934444

Figure 1.2.2　Supplier, Truck and Order Relations

RAW MATERIAL RELATION

Raw Material ID	Raw Material Name	QOH	Supplier ID
A	Water	9999	999
B	Cement paste	400	412
C	Sand	1200	444
D	Gravel	200	444
E	Marble	100	499
F	Shell	25	499

BILL OF MATERIAL RELATION

Concrete Type	Raw Material ID	Unit
1	B	1
1	C	2
1	A	1.5
2	B	1
2	C	2
2	A	1
3	B	1
3	C	2
3	A	1.5
3	D	3
4	B	1
4	C	2
4	A	1.5
4	E	2
5	B	1
5	C	2
5	A	1.5
5	F	2.5

Figure 1.2.3　Raw Material and Bill of Material Relations

- **Creating Solomon Enterprise Database**

Next, we will show how to create Solomon Enterprise Database, during which, we have to mention ***data dictionary***, which contains the logical structure for the information.

To create the Solomon Enterprise database, we have to do the following steps one by

1　Independent Experiment Guidance

one：

1. Start Microsoft Access 2016 (or other versions).
2. Select **Blank desktop database.**
3. Select a folder for the database and enter a file name (we'll use **Solomon Enterprises**).
4. Click on the **Create** button.

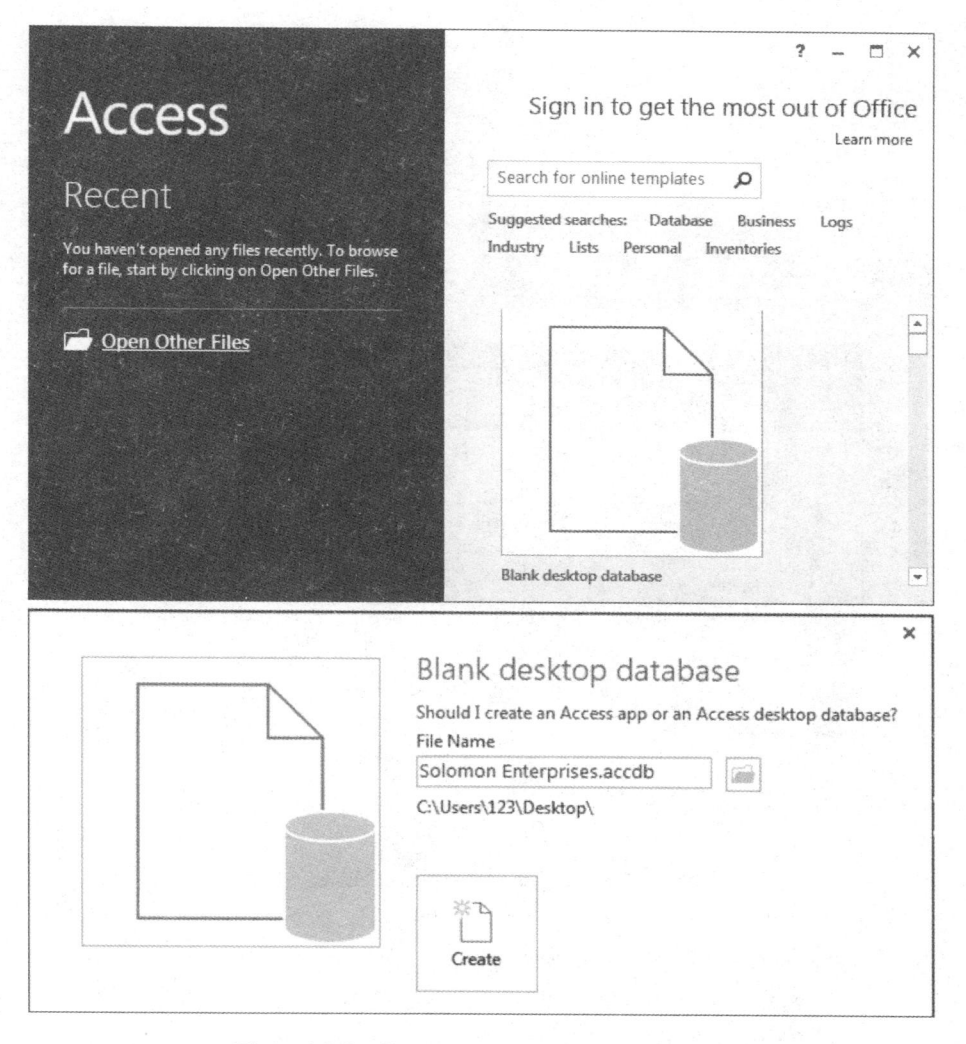

Figure 1.2.4　Create a New Database and Name it

To create a relation (table) in Design view：

1. Make sure the **Create** tab is selected and then double-click on the **Table Design** button.

2. Enter a name, data type, and description (the last is optional) for each field in a given relation.

3. Save that structure and repeat the process until you've created the structure for each relation in your database.

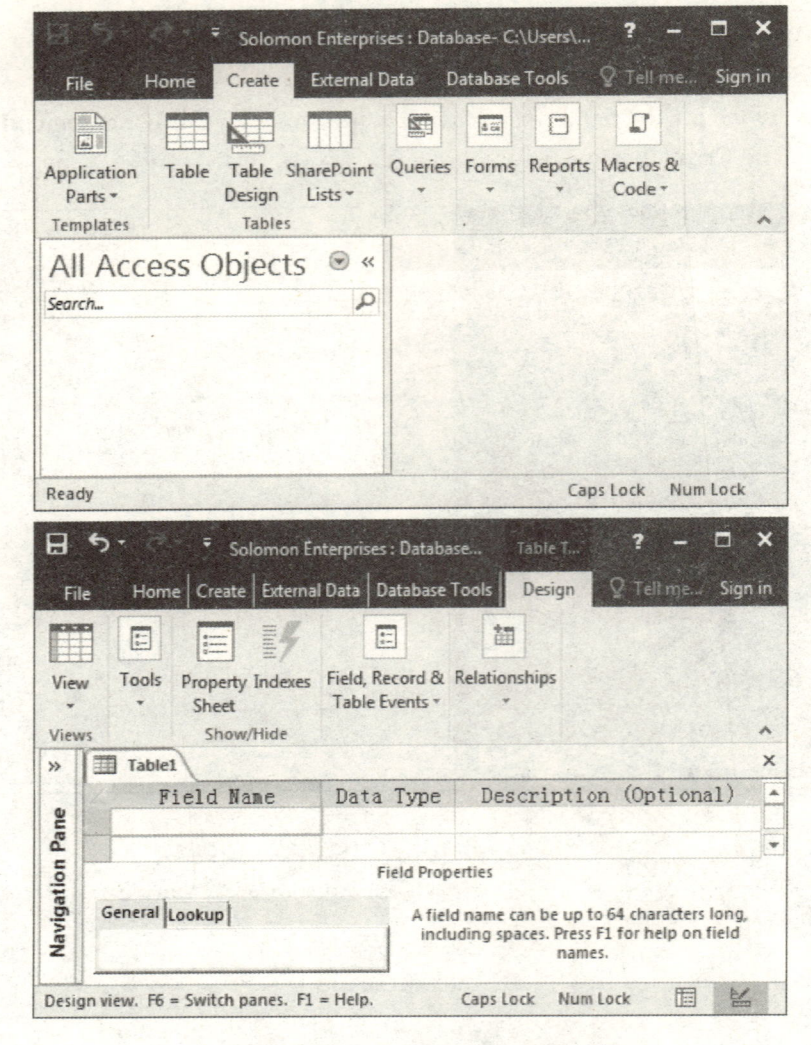

Figure 1.2.5　Create a Relation in Design View

　　Create the *Raw Material* Relation as follows:

　　1. Enter the four fields of the *Raw Material* relation, which are *Raw Material ID*, *Raw Material Name*, *QOH*, *Supplier ID*.

　　2. Click on the *Raw Material ID* row and then the key button to designate *Raw Material ID* as the primary key.

1 Independent Experiment Guidance

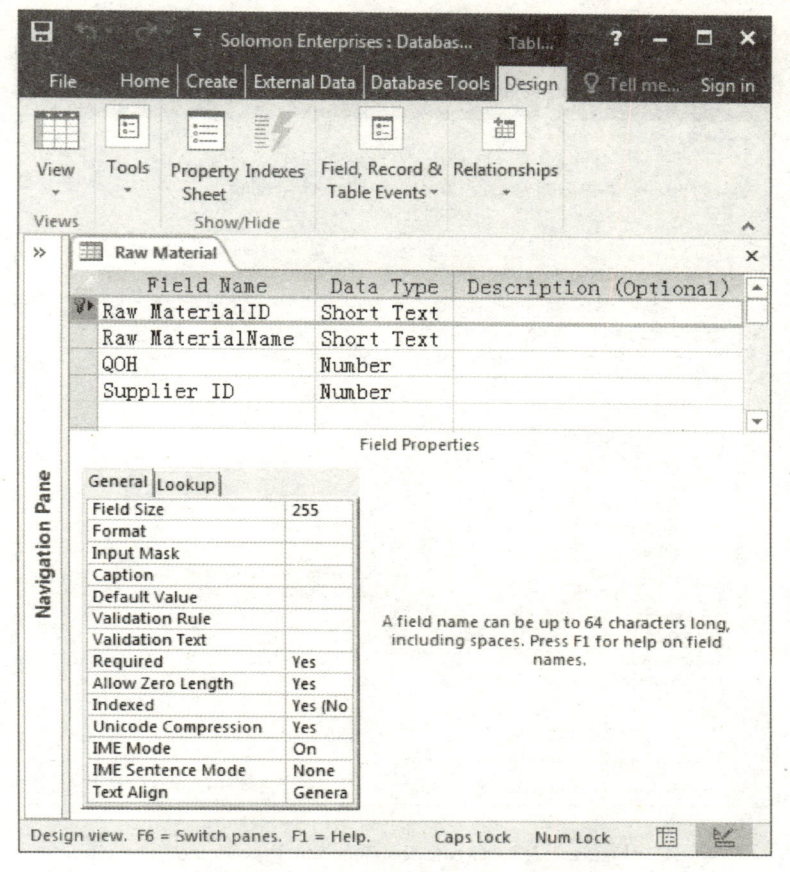

Figure 1.2.6 Create the Raw Material Relation

Create the *Concrete Type* Relation as follows.

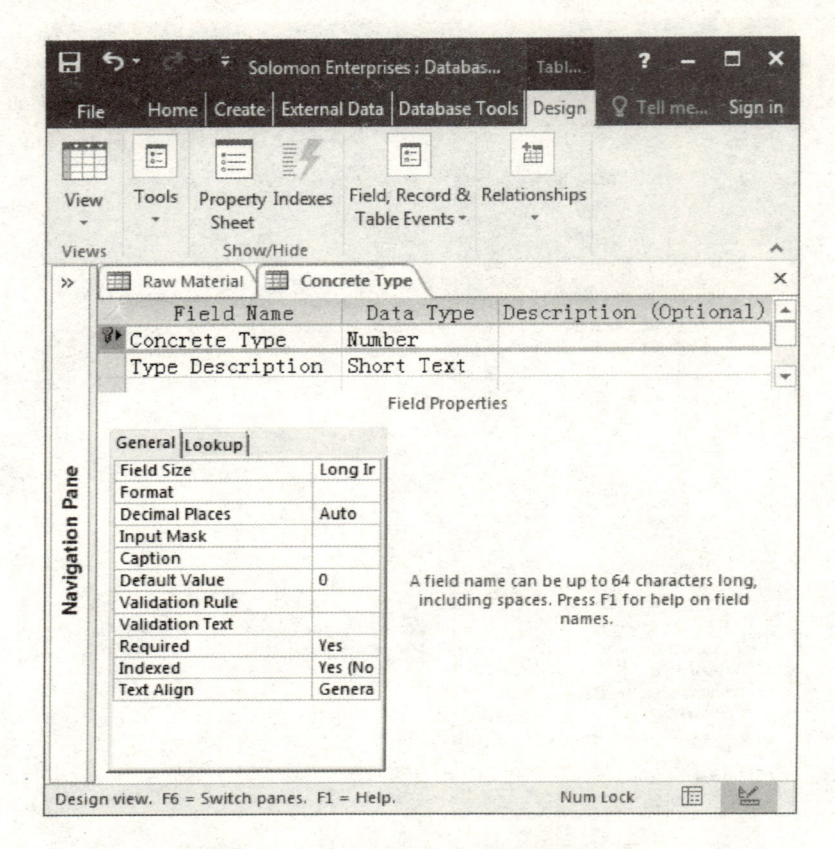

Figure 1.2.7 Create the Concrete Type Relation

Create the *Bill of Material* Relation as follows:

1. We create the *Bill of Material* Relation to eliminate the many-to-many relationship between the *Concrete Type and Raw Material* relations.

2. The *Bill of Material* Relation has a primary key composed of two fields (composite primary key):*Concrete Type* and *Raw Material ID*.

Composite primary key consists of the primary key fields from the two intersecting relations.

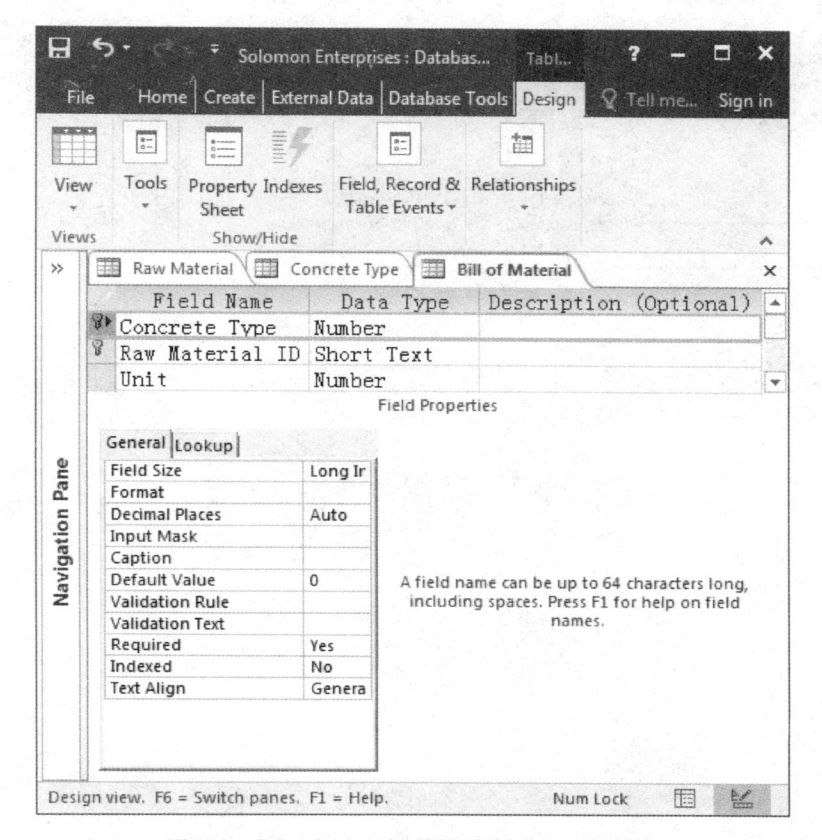

Figure 1.2.8 Create the Bill of Material Relation

Define relationships within Solomon Enterprise Database:

The final structural task is to define how all the relations relate to each other, that is, to link primary and foreign keys.

Foreign key is a primary key of one file (relation) that appears in another file (relation). Primary and Foreign Key Logical Ties are as the following.

CUSTOMER FILE
Customer Number – Primary Key

CONCRETE TYPE FILE
Concrete Type – Primary Key

ORDER FILE
Order Number – Primary Key
Customer Number – Foreign Key
Concrete Type – Foreign Key
Truck Number – Foreign Key
Driver ID – Foreign Key

TRUCK FILE
Truck Number – Primary Key

EMPLOYEE FILE
Employee ID – Primary Key

BILL OF MATERIAL FILE
Concrete Type
Raw Material ID } Composite Primary Key

RAW MATERIAL FILE
Raw Material ID – Primary Key
Supplier ID – Foreign Key

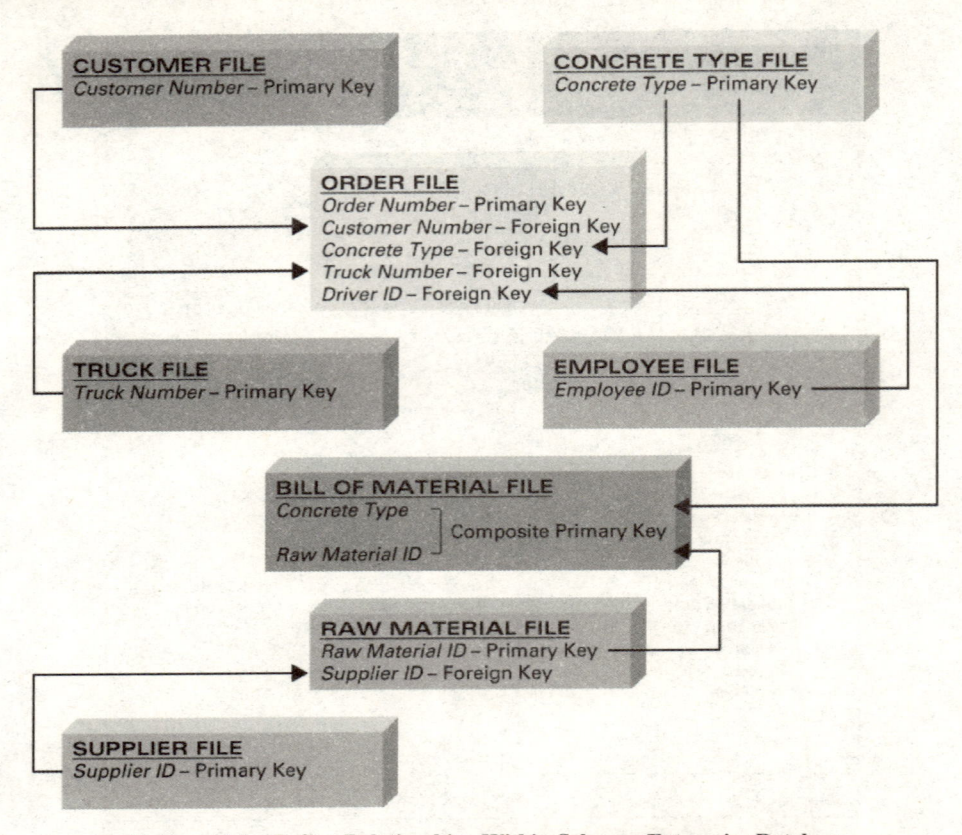

SUPPLIER FILE
Supplier ID – Primary Key

Figure 1.2.9　Define Relationships Within Solomon Enterprise Database

Define Relationships between Relations：

1. Click on the **Relationships** button in the button bar.

2. Make each relation appear on the palette by highlighting each relation name and clicking on the **Add** button.

3. Then click on the **Close** button.

4. You will have all the relations you chose，then define relationships between Relations by foreign keys.

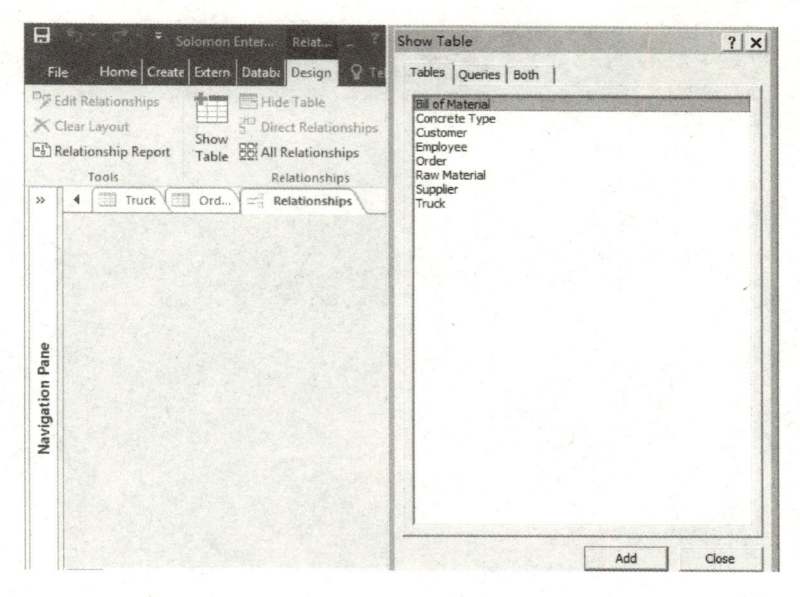

Figure 1.2.10　Choose Relations (tables)

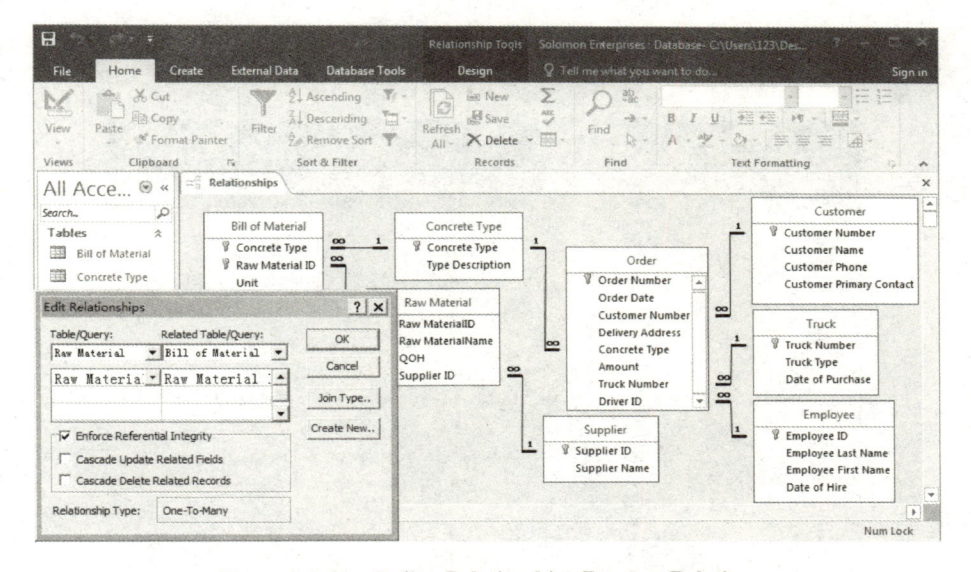

Figure 1.2.11　Define Relationships Between Relations

Enter information into Solomon Enterprise Database as follows:

1. To enter information, you simply highlight the desired relation and double-click on the mouse.

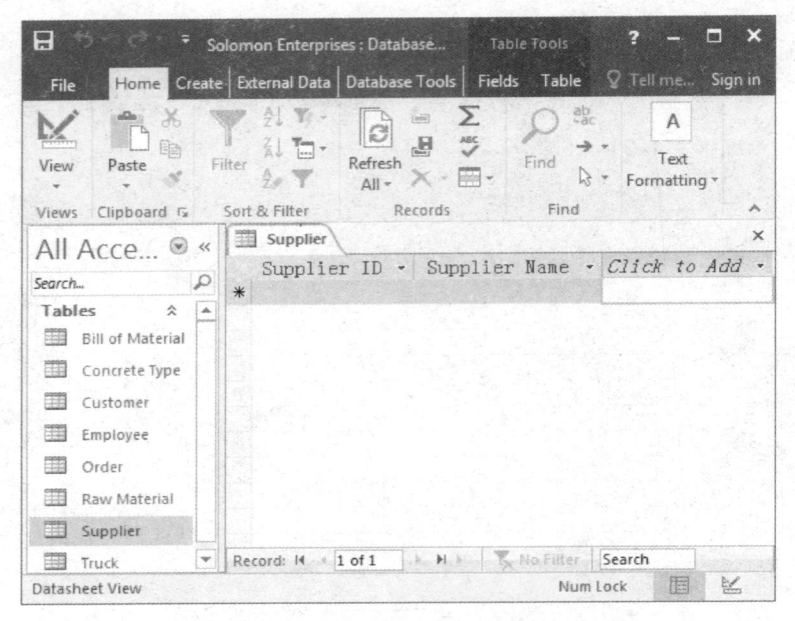

Figure 1.2.12 Open Supplier Relation

2. Enter Information.

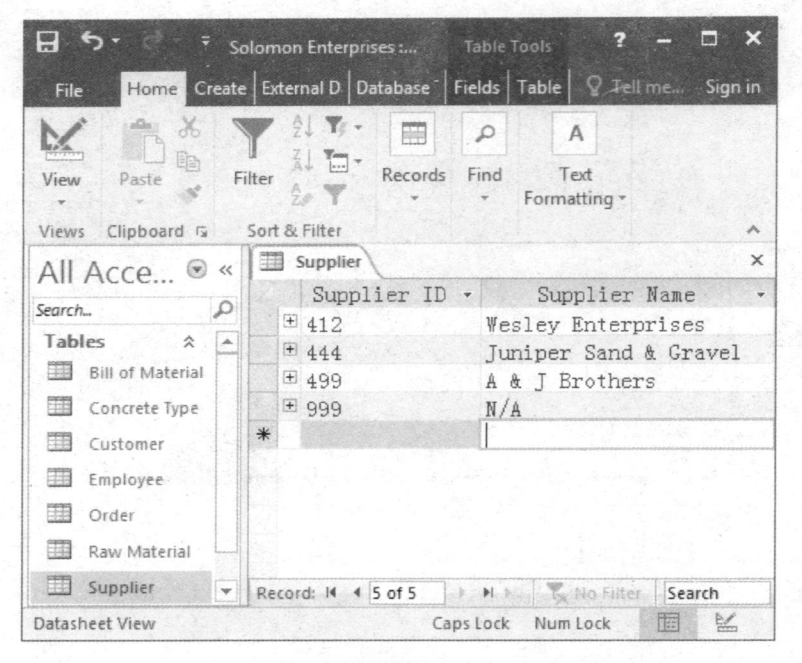

Figure 1.2.13 Enter Information

1 Independent Experiment Guidance

Referential integrity:

Referential integrity ensures consistency. For example, that you don't put a non-existent *Supplier ID* into the *Raw Material* relation. The relationships we set up for referential integrity guard against bad information.

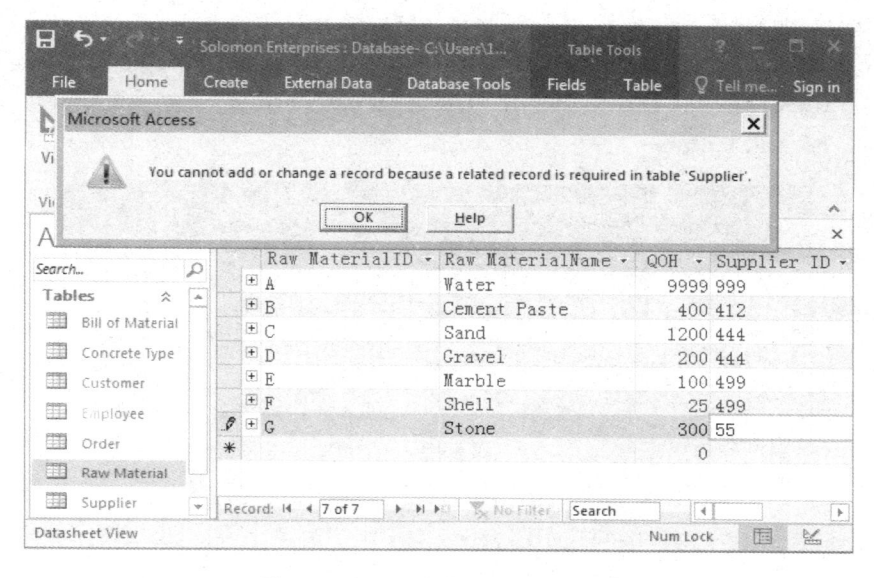

Figure 1.2.14 Referential Integrity

Change the Structure of a Relation as follows:

Highlight the relation and right-click on the mouse and choose **Design View**, or you can click on the **View-Design View** button on the left of the toolbar.

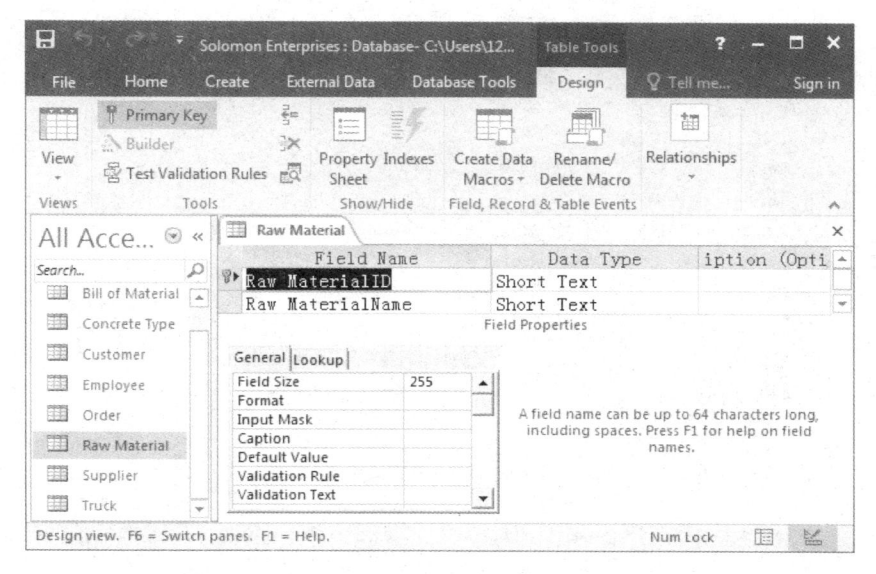

Figure 1.2.15 Change the Structure of a Relation

Create a simple query using one relation:

Query-by-example (QBE) tool — help you graphically design the answer to a question. Suppose we want to see a list of raw materials that shows:

- ✓ *Raw Material Name*
- ✓ *Supplier ID*

Create a Simple Query Using the Raw Material Relation as follows. Firstly find the QBE tool, click on the **Create** tab menu, then the **Query Design** button. Then, highlight the relations and click on the **Add button**.

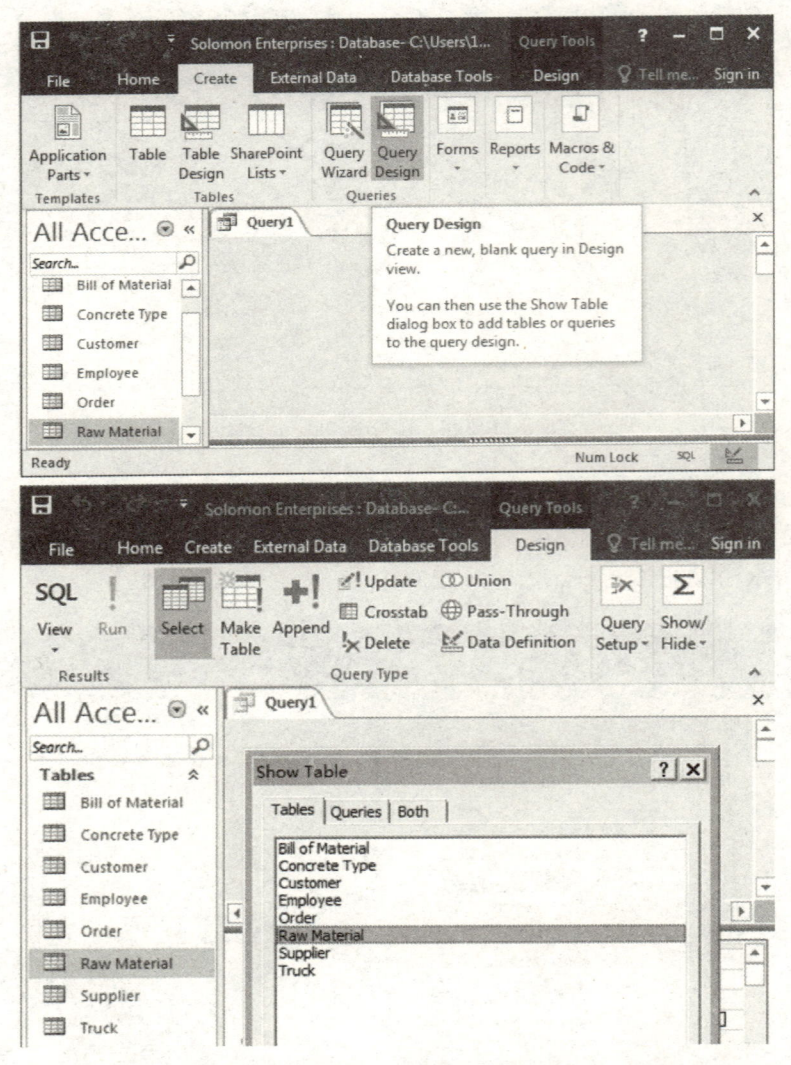

Figure 1.2.16 Create a Simple Query Using One Relation — Choose Table

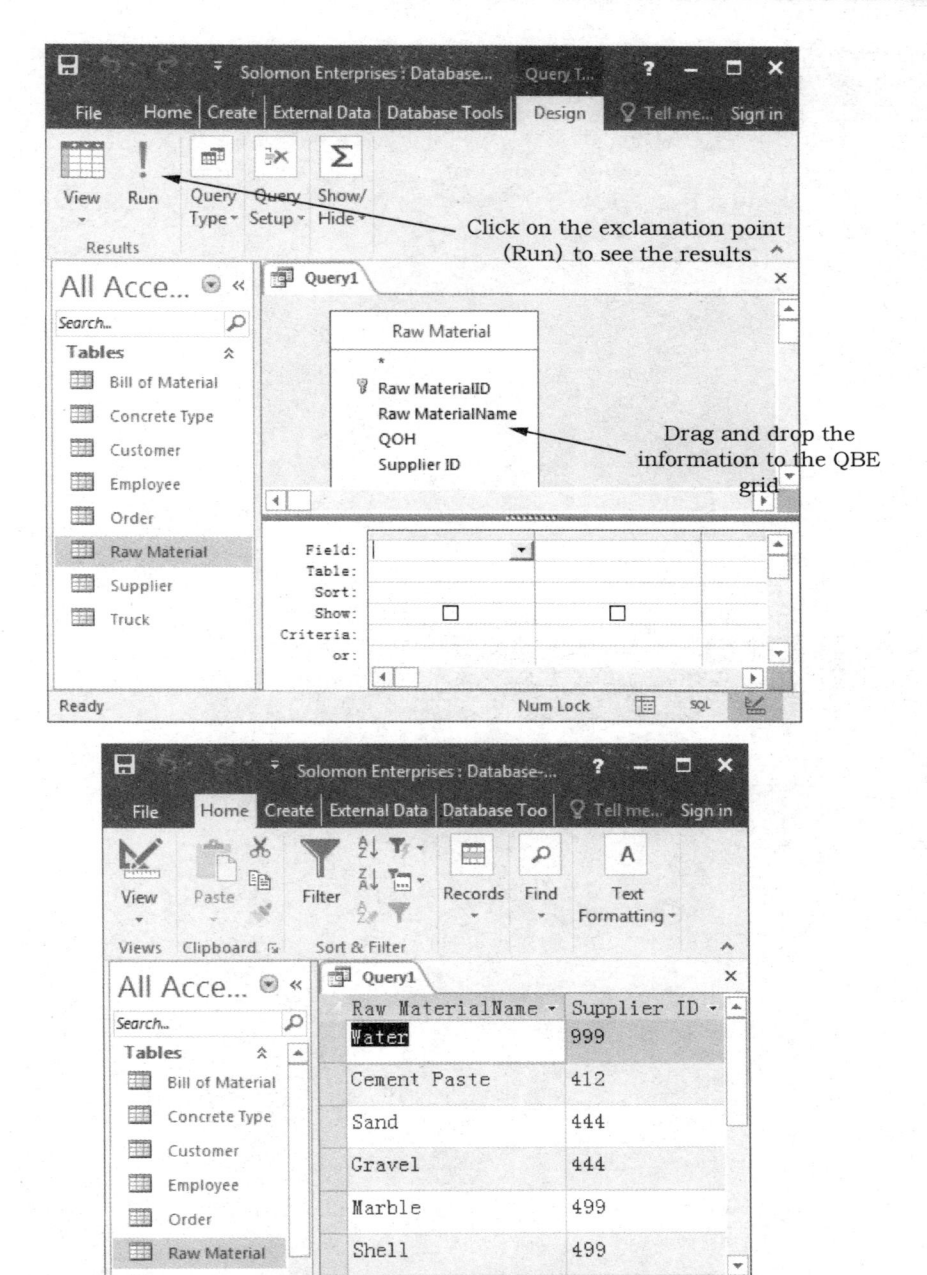

Figure 1.2.17　Create a Simple Query Using One Relation — Show the Result

Create a Simple Query with a Condition as follows.

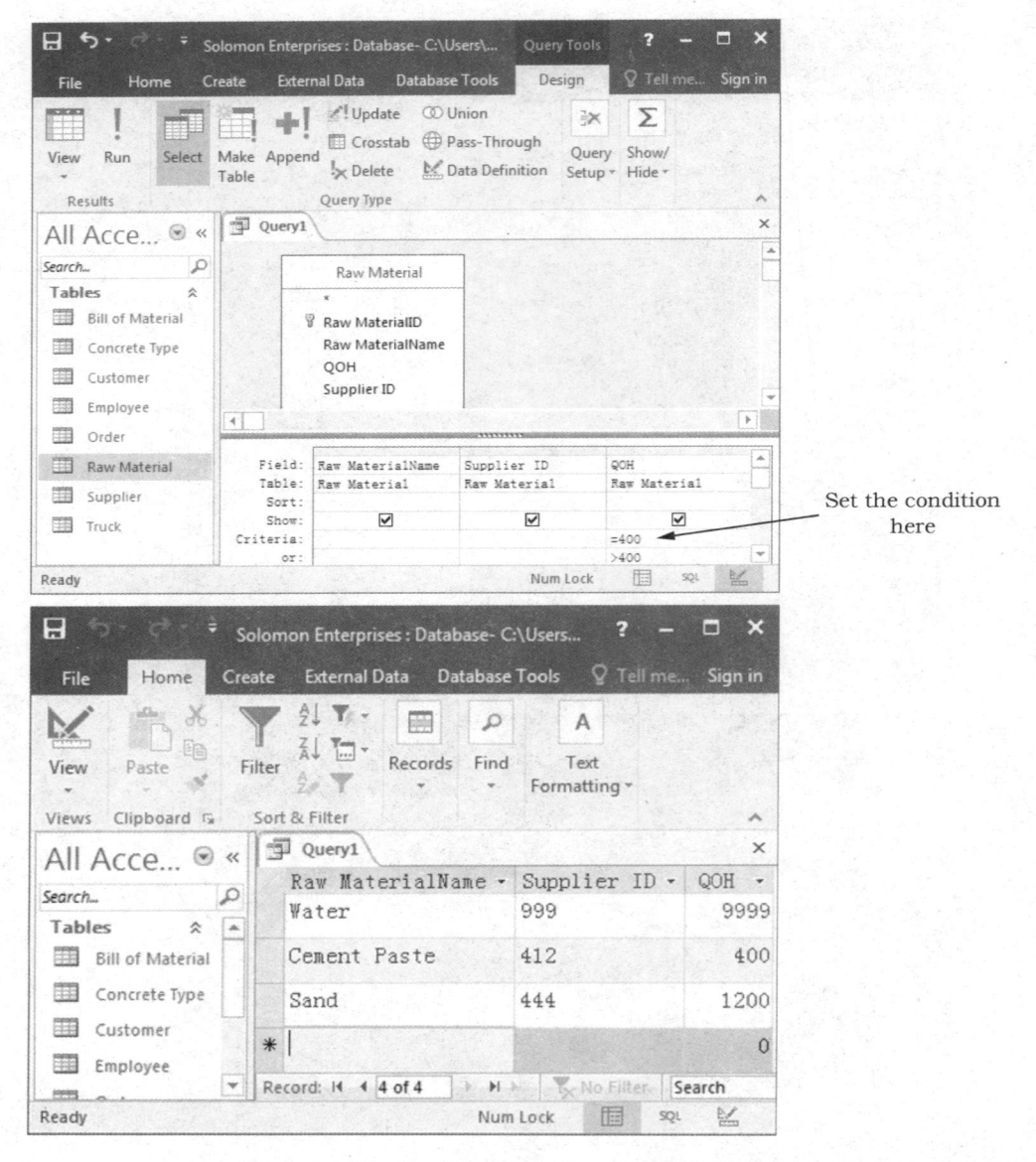

Figure 1.2.18   Create a Simple Query with a Condition

Create an advanced query using more than one relation. Suppose we want a query that shows all order numbers, date of orders, where the goods were delivered, the contact person, the truck involved in each delivery, and the truck driver in each delivery.

Steps to create an advanced query as follows:

1. Select the **Create** tab and double-click on **Query Design**.

2. Right click on the mouse, in the **Show Table** dialog box:

(1) Select and **Add** the relation names.

(2) Close the **Show Table** dialog box.

Tables linked appear are joined by lines with 1 beside the table with the primary key,

1　Independent Experiment Guidance

and the infinity sign by the table with the foreign key.

3. Drag and drop the fields that you want from the appropriate relation into the QBE grid in the order that you want.

4. Click on the exclamation point (**Run**) in the button bar to see the results of the query.

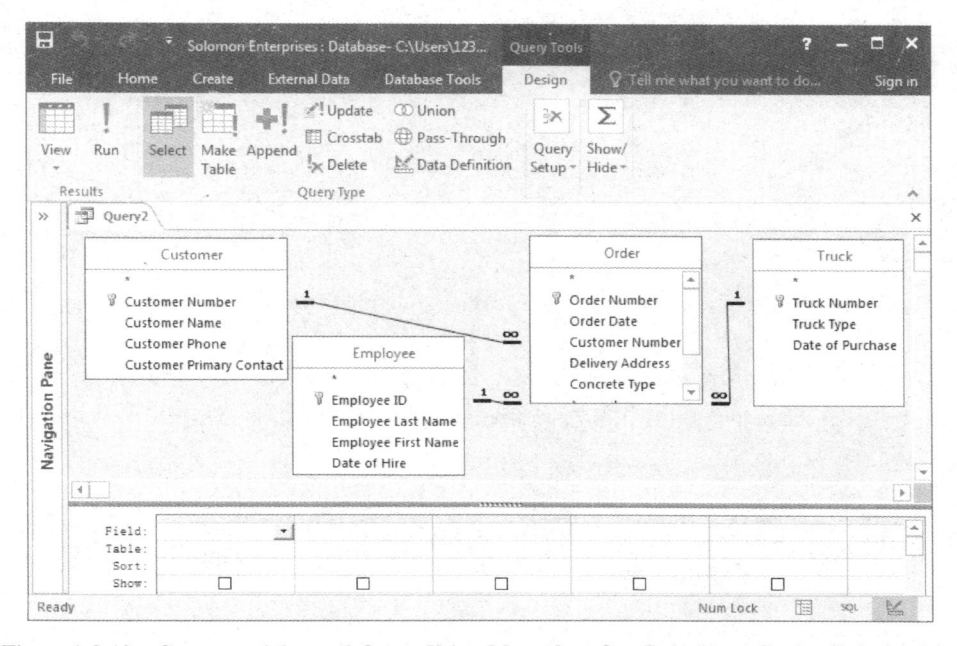

Figure 1.2.19　Create an Advanced Query Using More than One Relation — Design Relationships

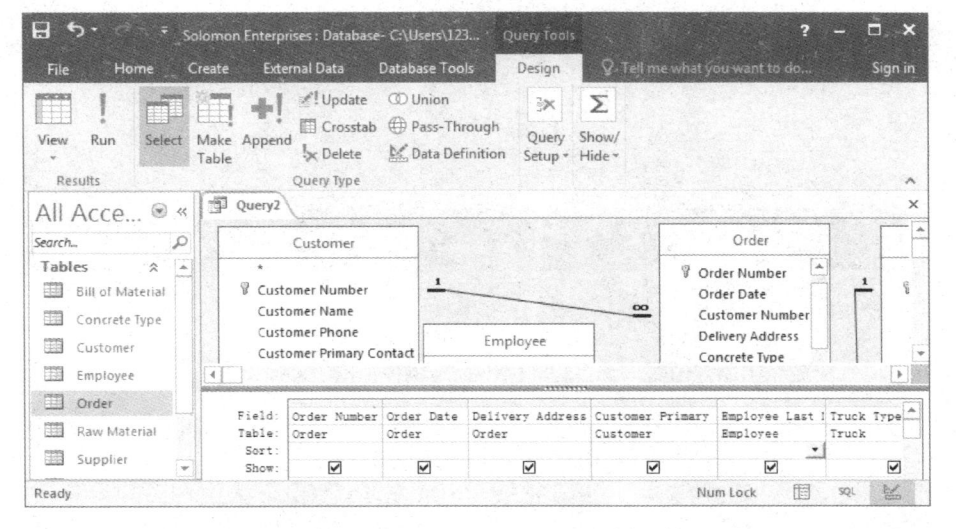

Figure 1.2.20　Create an Advanced Query Using More than One Relation — Design Query Conditions

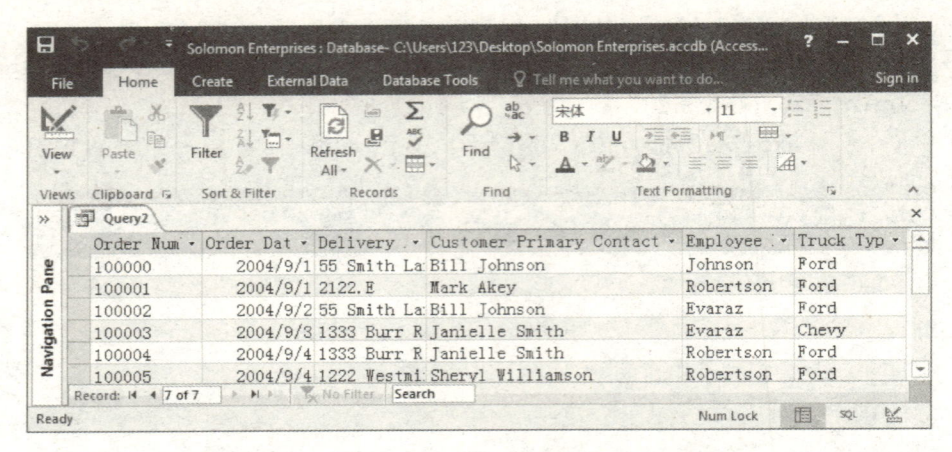

Figure 1.2.21　Create an Advanced Query Using More than One Relation — Query Result

To generate a simple report based some relations or queries, firstly open this relation or query, click on the **Create** menu, then the **Report** button. We take the Customer relation to show the result.

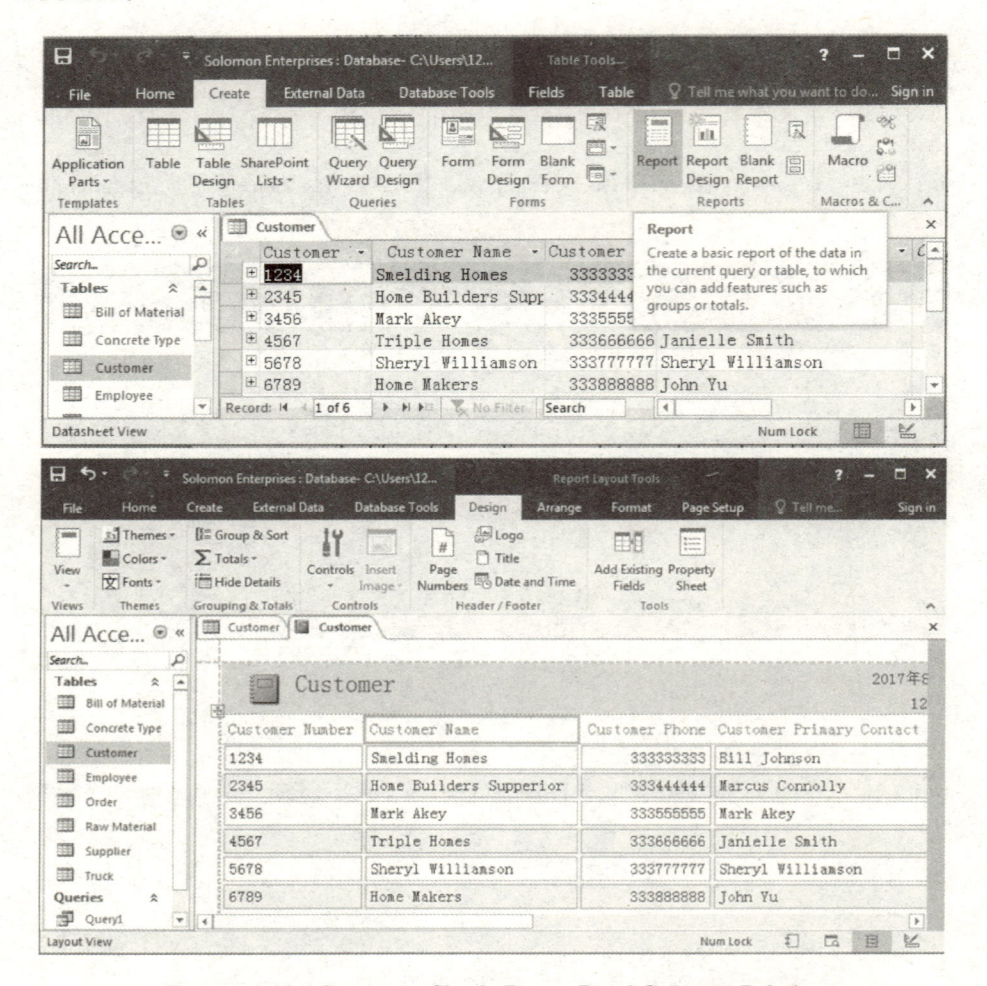

Figure 1.2.22　Generate a Simple Report Based Customer Relation

You could also right click on the mouse, and choose **Design View** to design the report structure. Steps to adjust the report to make it aesthetically pleasing are as follows:

1. Adjust the boxes to the desired size.

2. Delete unwanted entries.

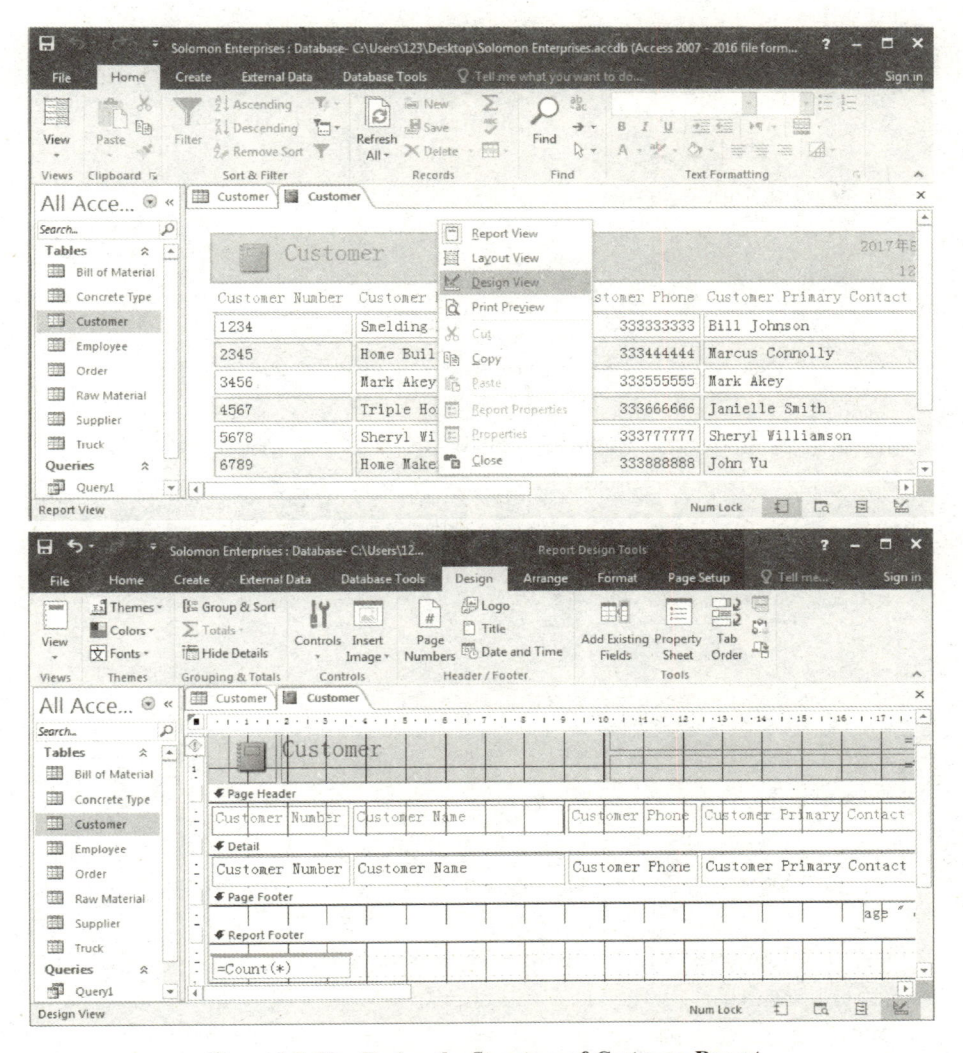

Figure 1.2.23   Design the Structure of Customer Report

You could create a new blank report by **Blank Report** button of **Create** menu, you can insert fields and control and design the report.

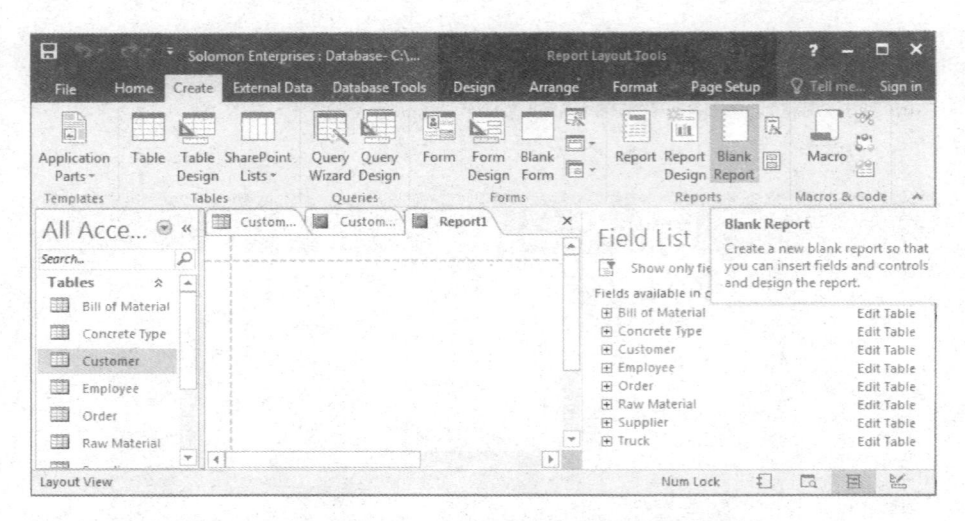

Figure 1.2.24　Design a New Report by Blank Report Button

Create a report by using the **Report Wizard** button of the **Create** menu.

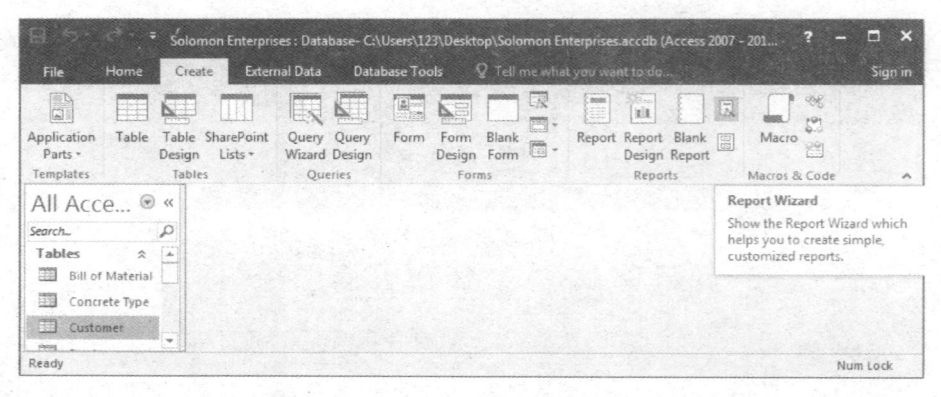

Figure 1.2.25　Design a New Report by Report Wizard Button

The steps are as follows if using **Report Wizard** to have a report：
1. Choose tables and/or queries：Let you choose which table/query you want.
2. Choose fields：Let you choose the fields you want.
3. Grouping,Sorting,Layout of Report.
Grouping：Let you specify grouping of information.
Sorting：Allow you to specify sorting.
Layout and orientation：Allow you to select layout and page orientation.
4. Style and Title.
Style：Allow you to choose from among predefined report styles.
Title：Name the report.

Let us design a report to show all customers and phone numbers. Following the steps of **Report Wizard** one by one,then you can have a report perhaps as the following：

1 Independent Experiment Guidance

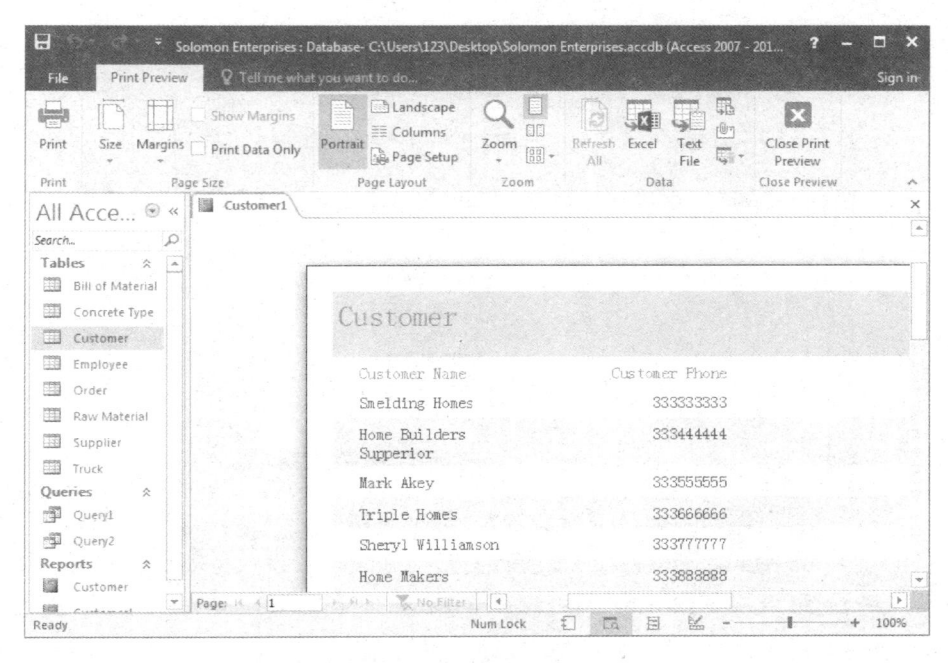

Figure 1.2.26   Show the Report

Create a data input form to let you enter information for a record at a time, just like a report, which has the following ways:

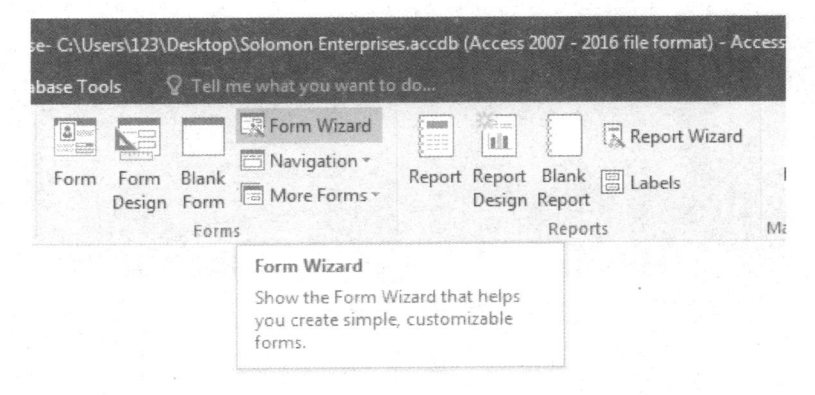

Figure 1.2.27   Ways of Creating a Form

Here show how to use **Form Wizard** to create a Form:
1. Click on **Form wizard**.
2. Choose **Table: Order**.
3. Select all the fields of the *Order table*.
Choose Table/Query and Fields.

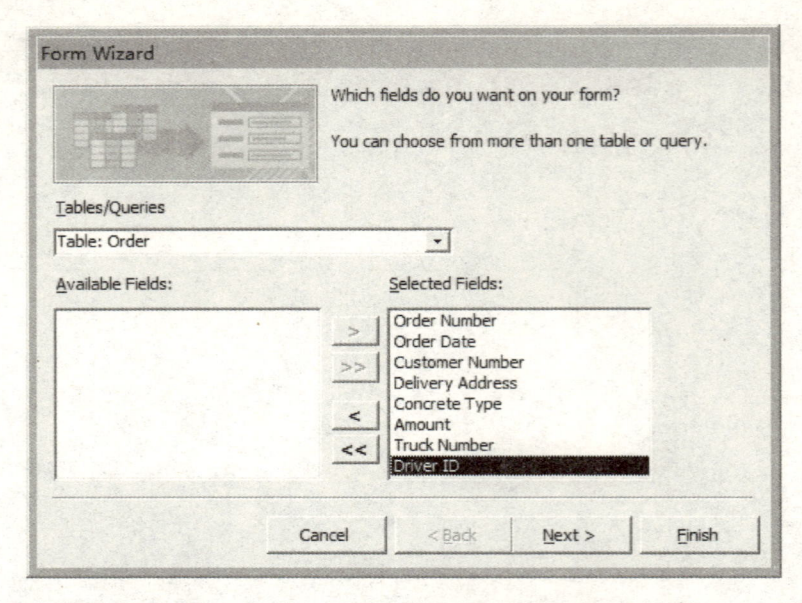

Figure 1.2.28 Create Form by Using Form Wizard and Choosing Table/Query and Fields

Choose Layout and Title:

You can choose a layout for your input Form.

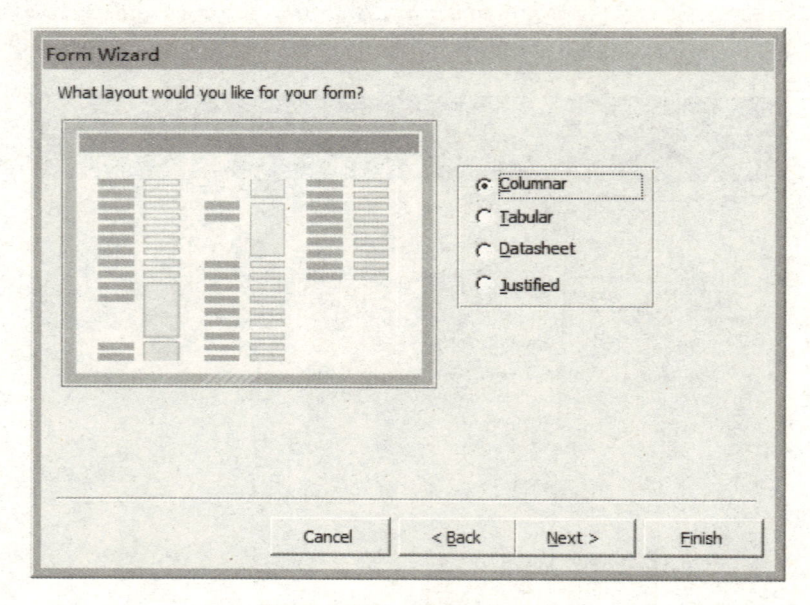

Figure 1.2.29 Choose Layout

Enter a title for the input Form and click on the **Finish** button.

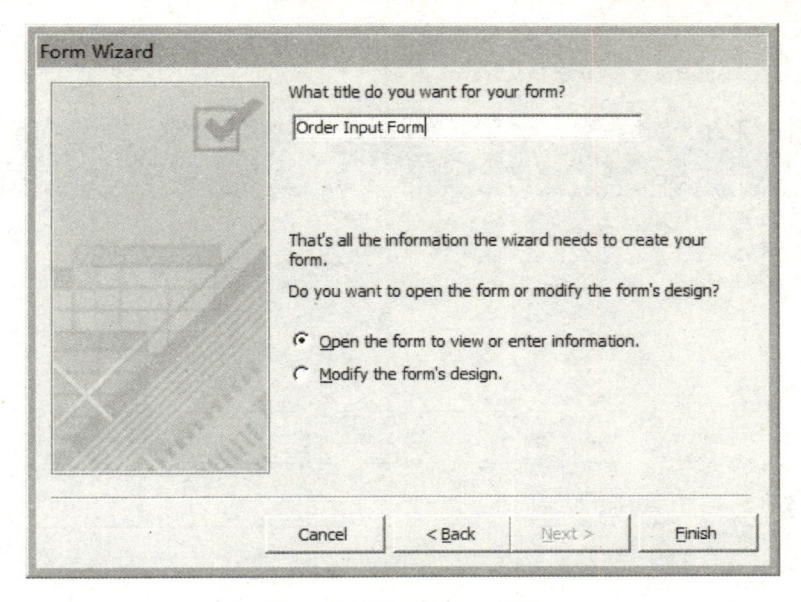

Figure 1.2.30 Enter a Title

Final Input Form is as follows.

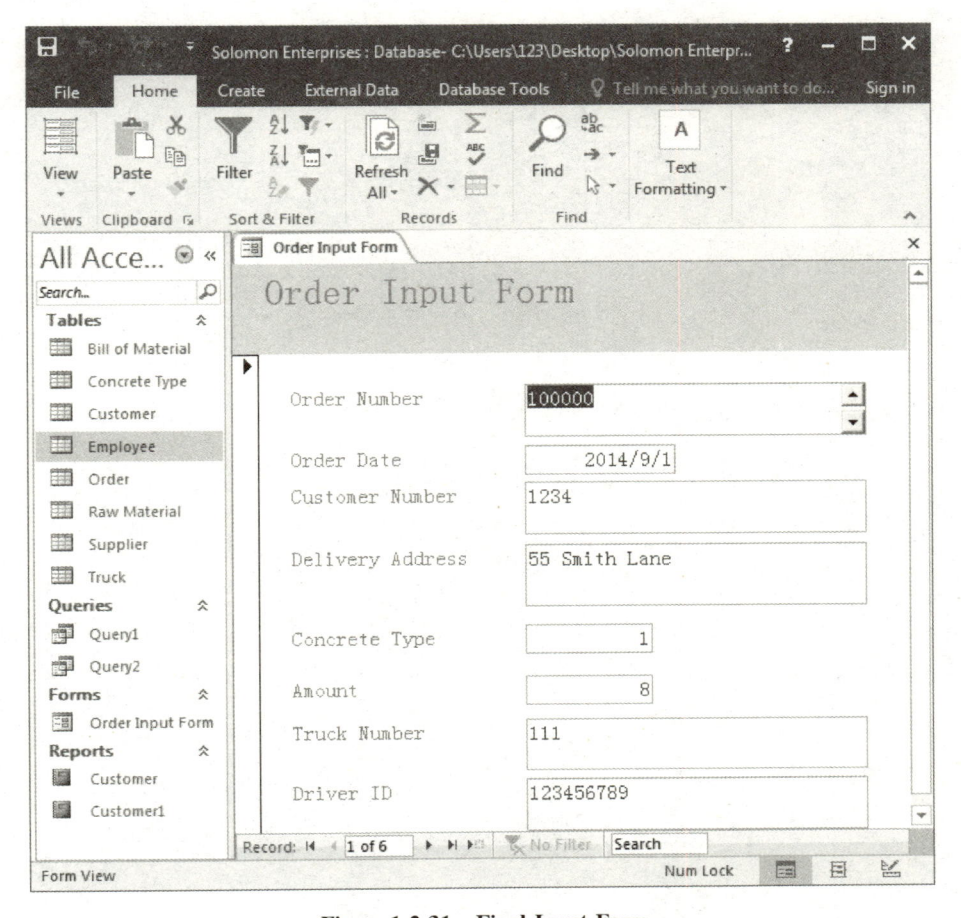

Figure 1.2.31 Final Input Form

If you are not satisfied with it, you can refine it by **Design View**, which occurs on the pop-up menu when right clicking on the mouse.

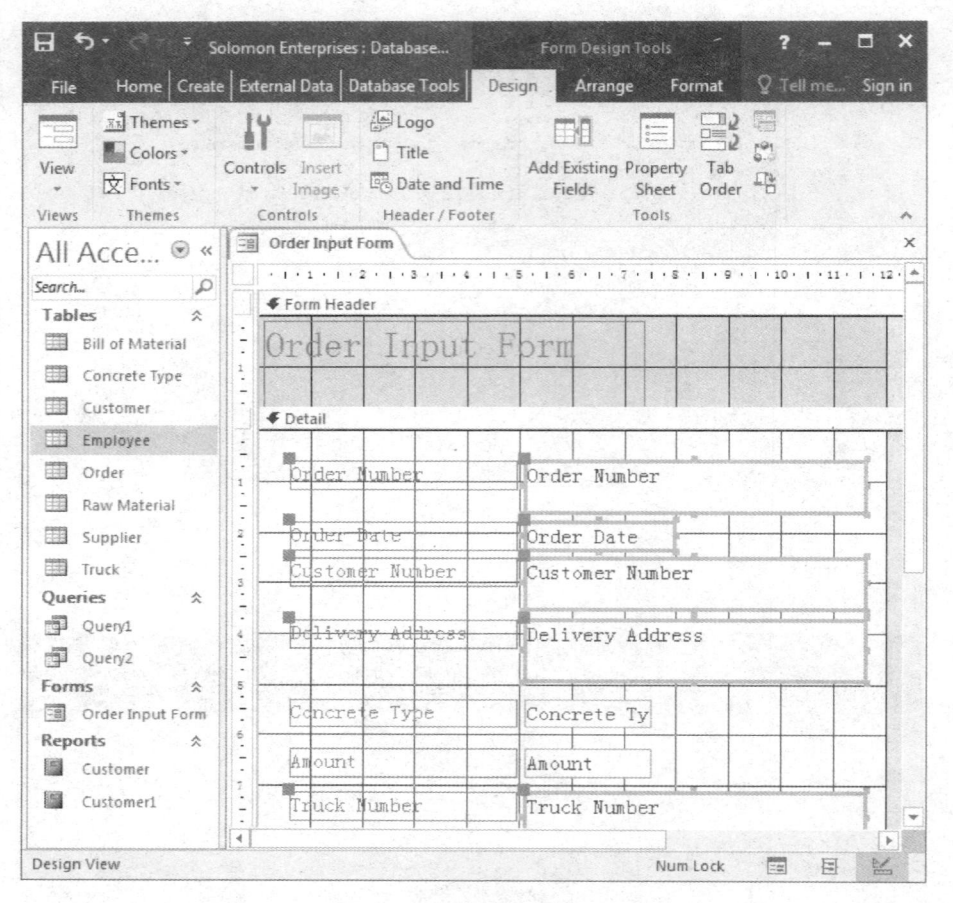

Figure 1.2.32　Refine a Form

Independent Experiment Guidance 3: Operating DSS Systems

● **Introduction**

IT plays an important role in aiding decision-making. Spreadsheet tools can aid in decision-making using some functions as follows:

1. List
2. AutoFilter
3. Conditional formatting
4. Pivot tables

● **List**

List — information arranged in columns and rows, which has the following characteristics:

1. Each column has one type of information
2. First row contains headings or labels
3. No blank rows
4. Blank columns/rows all around

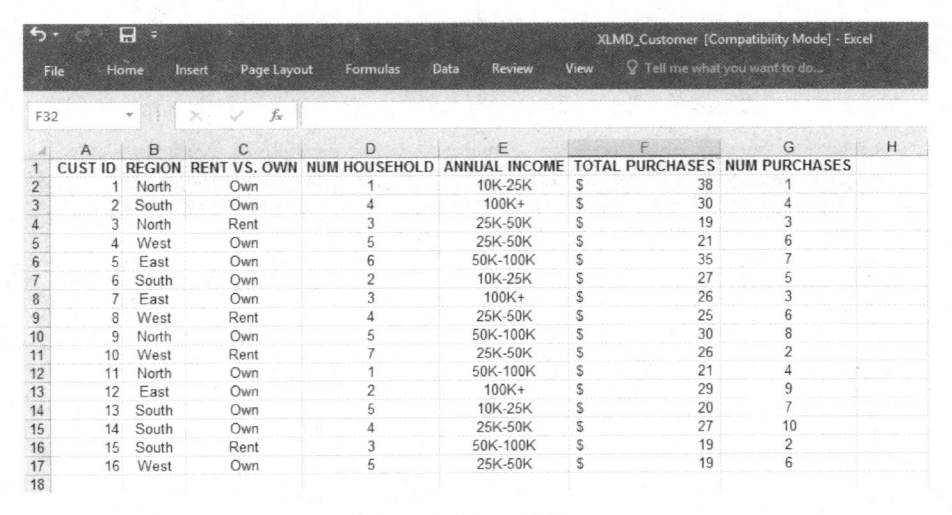

CUST ID	REGION	RENT VS. OWN	NUM HOUSEHOLD	ANNUAL INCOME	TOTAL PURCHASES	NUM PURCHASES
1	North	Own	1	10K-25K	$ 38	1
2	South	Own	4	100K+	$ 30	4
3	North	Rent	3	25K-50K	$ 19	3
4	West	Own	5	25K-50K	$ 21	6
5	East	Own	6	50K-100K	$ 35	7
6	South	Own	2	10K-25K	$ 27	5
7	East	Own	3	100K+	$ 26	3
8	West	Rent	4	25K-50K	$ 25	6
9	North	Own	5	50K-100K	$ 30	8
10	West	Rent	7	25K-50K	$ 26	2
11	North	Own	1	50K-100K	$ 21	4
12	East	Own	2	100K+	$ 29	9
13	South	Own	5	10K-25K	$ 20	7
14	South	Own	4	25K-50K	$ 27	10
15	South	Rent	3	50K-100K	$ 19	2
16	West	Own	5	25K-50K	$ 19	6

Figure 1.3.1 List

List definition table — description of a list by column, such as:

✓ *CUST ID* — Unique ID for customer
✓ *REGION* — North, South, etc.
✓ *RENT VS. OWN* — customer rents or owns a home

● **Filter**

Filter function — filter a list and hide rows that don't match criteria, which is good for seeing only certain rows of information. Filter supports only "equal to" criteria.

Example：Find the customers in the North *REGION*.

Filter steps：

1. Open workbook (**XLMD_Customer.xls** from www.mhhe.com/haag).

2. Click in any cell in the list.

3. Menu bar—click on **Data**,point at **Filter**.

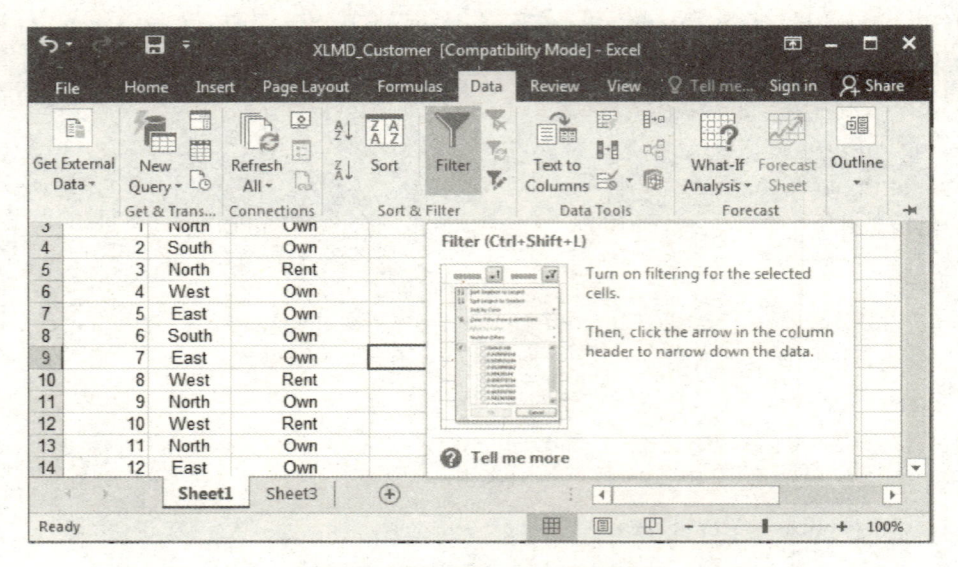

Figure 1.3.2　Find the AutoFilter

Click **Filter**,we will see list box arrows next to each label or column heading.

Figure 1.3.3　Pull-down Arrow Occurs

Each column will have a pull-down arrow. Click on it and select the criteria.

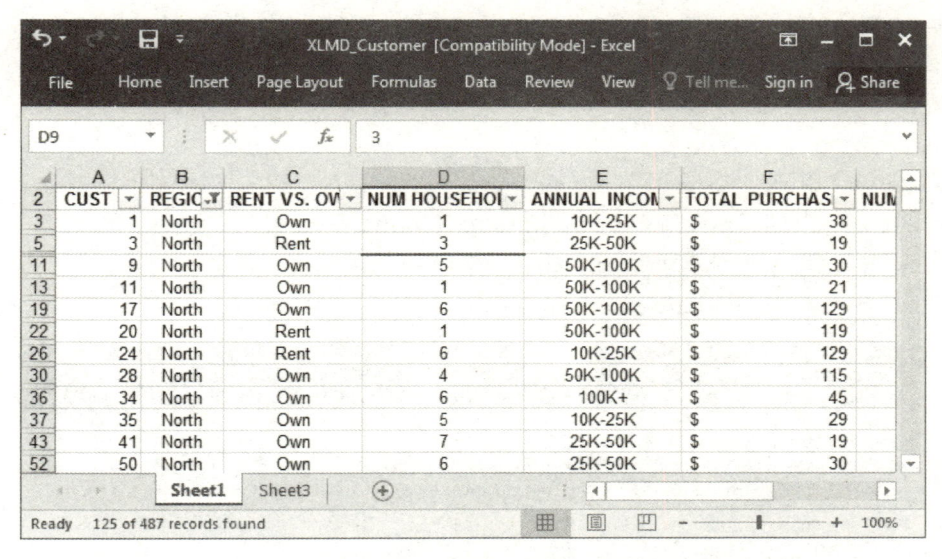

Figure 1.3.4 Result of Meeting Some Selection Criteria

Excel will respond by showing only those records that meet the selection criteria.
Steps of turning off Filter from Menu bar:
- ✓ Click on **Data**
- ✓ Click **Filter**

Filter can also filter on multiple columns, for example:
- ✓ Customers in North region (select North in *REGION*)
- ✓ Own a home (select Own in *RENT VS. OWN*)
- ✓ Only one household member (select 1 in *NUM HOUSEHOLD*)

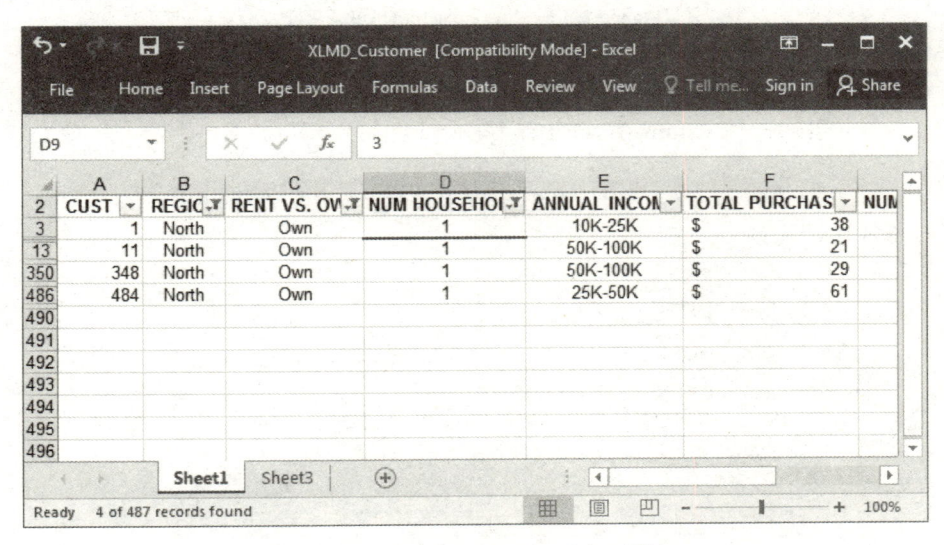

Figure 1.3.5 One Example of AutoFilter

- **Custom AutoFilter**

Custom AutoFilter function — hide all rows except those that meet criteria, besides "is equal to", for example: Customers with more than 3 household members.

Custom AutoFilter Steps:

1. Turn on Filter.

2. Click on pull-down arrow in appropriate column.

3. Complete Custom AutoFilter dialog box with criteria.

4. Click on the **OK button**.

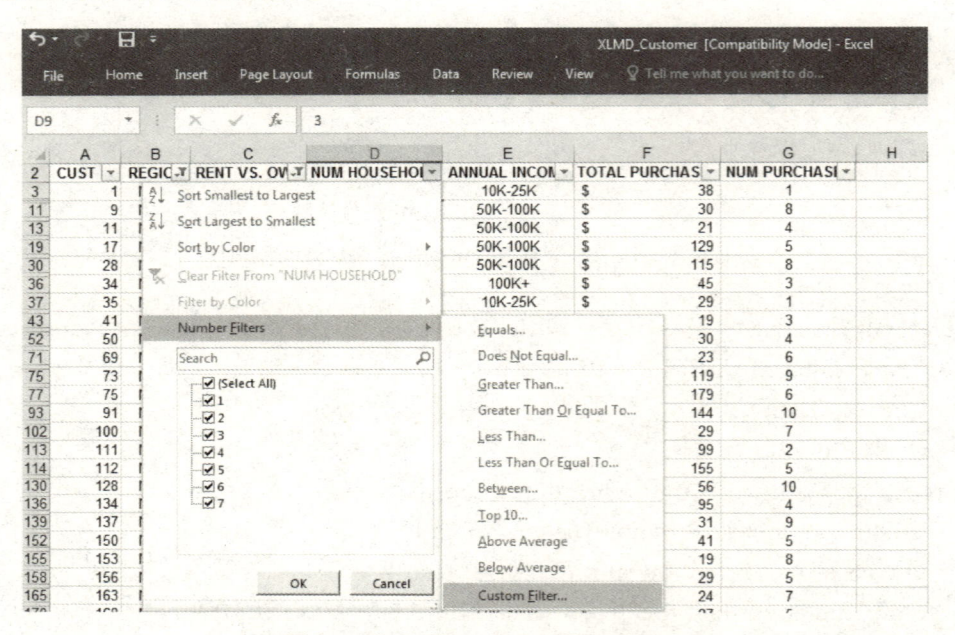

Figure 1.3.6　Start Custom AutoFilter

To use Custom AutoFilter, click on the appropriate pull-down arrow and select (**Custom Filter…**), you will see a **Custom AutoFilter** box.

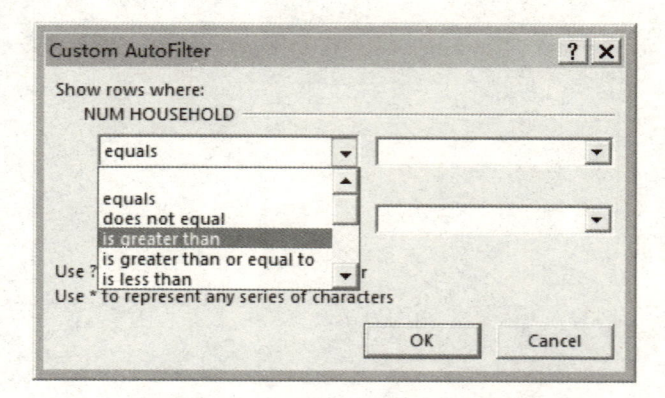

Figure 1.3.7　Custom AutoFilter Box

Choose the appropriate logical operation.

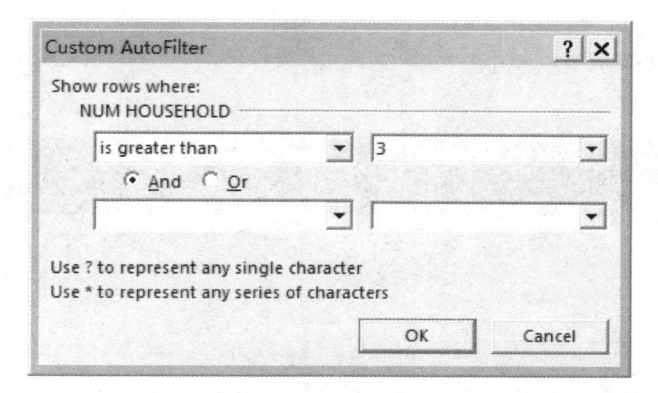

Figure 1.3.8 Choose the Appropriate Logical Operation

Enter the appropriate value and click on **OK**. Excel will respond by presenting only the records that meet the selection criteria.

Figure 1.3.9 The Filtered Result

- **Conditional Formatting**

Conditional formatting — highlight the information in a cell that meets some criteria, whose characteristics are as follows:

1. Does not hide any rows.
2. The whole list can be seen.
3. Highlight certain information.

For example: Customers show purchased more than $100.

Conditional Formatting Steps:

1. Select entire appropriate column.
2. From the menu bar, click on **Home** and then **Conditional Formatting**.

3. Enter criteria.
4. Click on **Format...** and enter highlighting desired.
5. Click on **OK** twice.

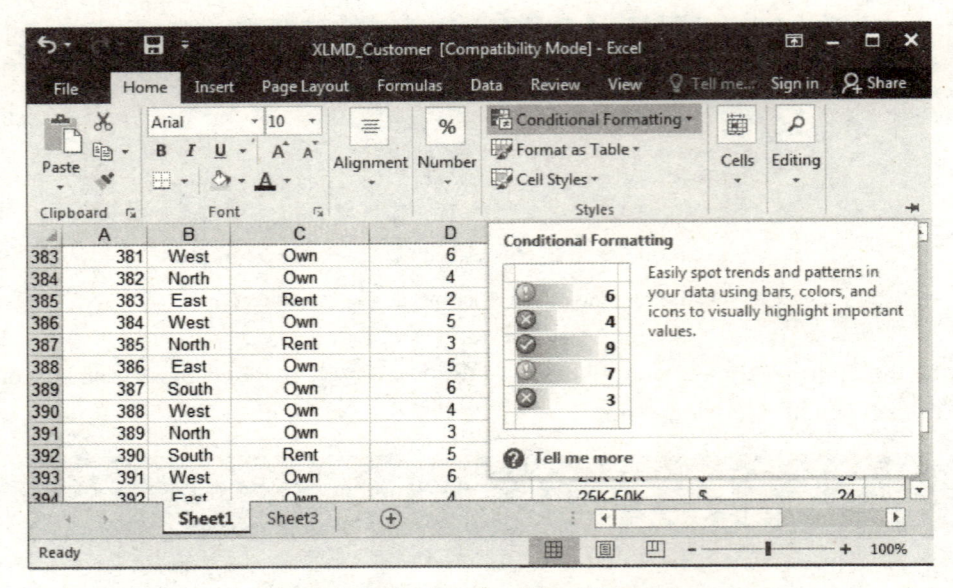

Figure 1.3.10 Start Conditional Formatting

First, highlight the appropriate column, from the menu bar, click on **Home** and then **Conditional Formatting**, then **New Rule**….

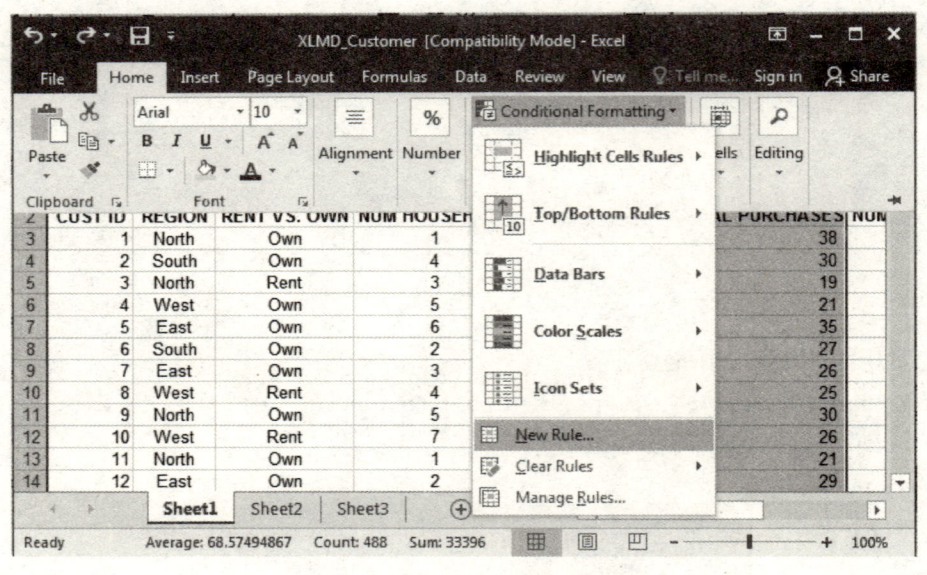

Figure 1.3.11 Find New Rule

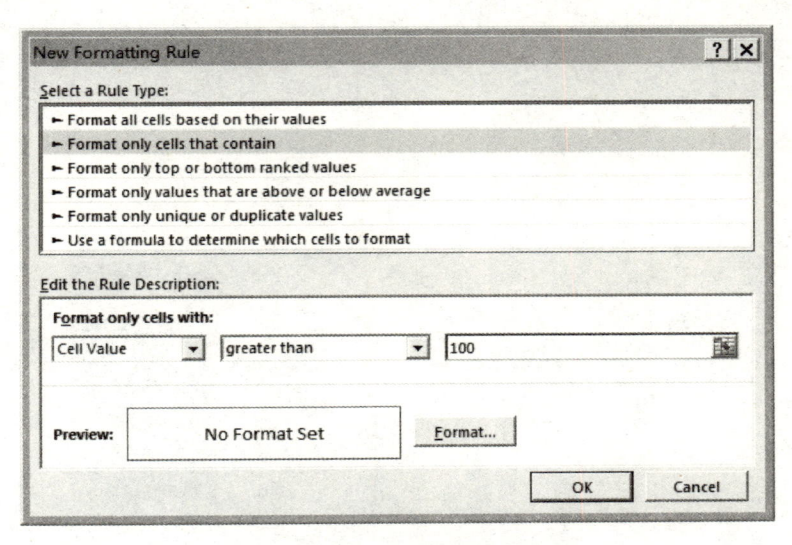

Figure 1.3.12 Set the Condition

In the **New Formatting Rule** box, select the logical operator, enter the appropriate value, and click on **Format**.

Figure 1.3.13 Set the Pattern

Next, enter the formatting of your choice and click on **OK** twice.

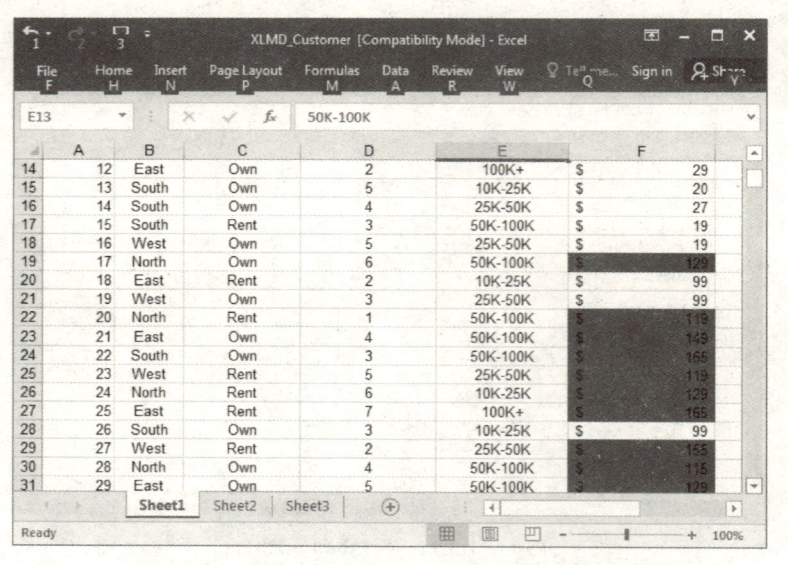

Figure 1.3.14　Show the Result of Conditional Formatting

Excel will highlight those cells meeting your selection criteria.

Steps of removing Conditional Formatting are as the following.

1. Highlight entire column with formatting.

2. From Menu bar, click on **Home** and then **Conditional Formatting**.

3. Click on **Clear Rules**.

4. Select appropriate next item.

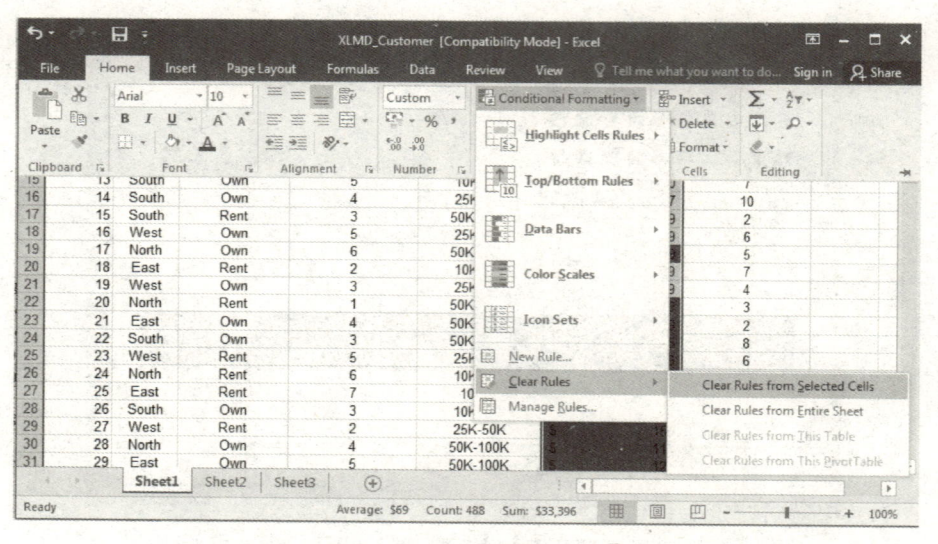

Figure 1.3.15　Remove Conditional Formatting

● **Pivot Tables**

Pivot tables — enable you to group and summarize information, the characteristics of which are as the following:

1. Show summaries of information by dimension.
2. Can be two-dimensional(2D).
3. Can be three-dimensional(3D).

2D Pivot Table

To create a 2D pivot table, click anywhere in list, from the menu bar click on **Insert**, and **Tables** and **PivotTable**.

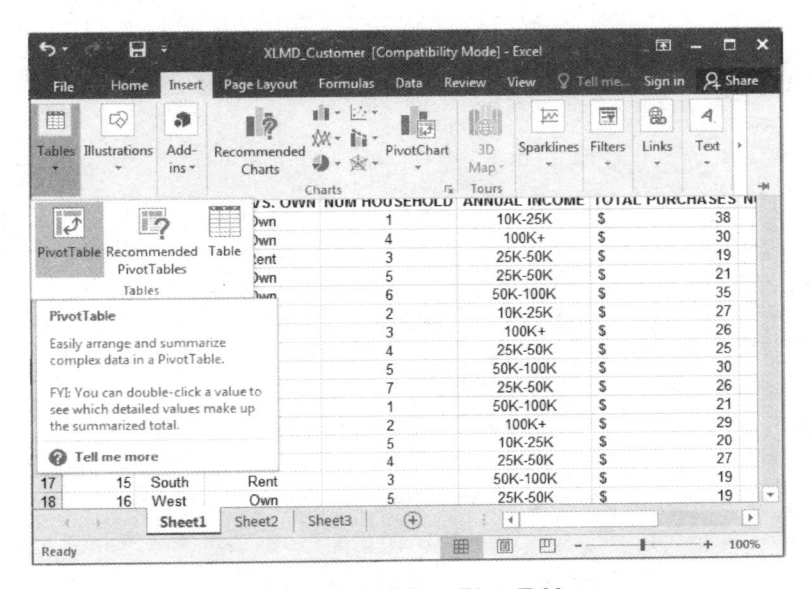

Figure 1.3.16 Start Pivot Table

Choose the data that you want to analyze and where you want the PivotTable report to be placed.

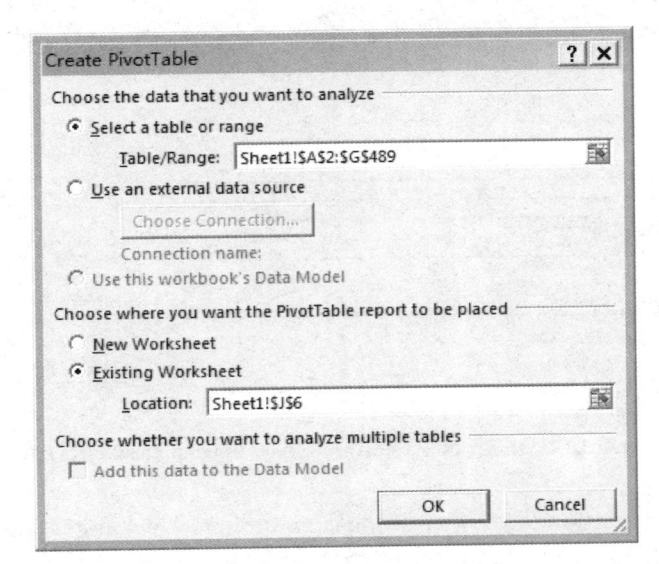

Figure 1.3.17 Choose Data Source and Location for PivotTable Report

Click on **OK**, you will have blank PivotTable.

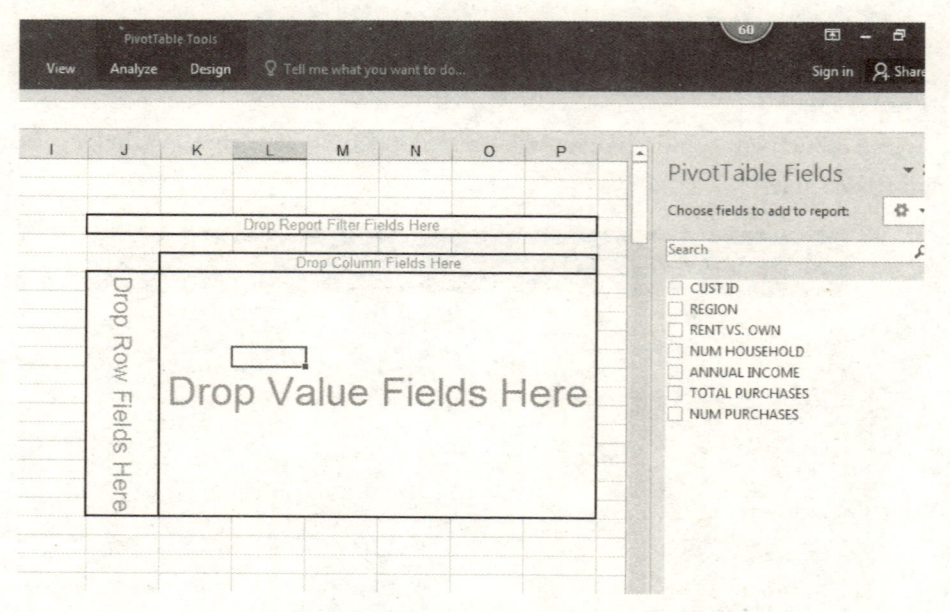

Figure 1.3.18   Blank PivotTable

Now, drag and drop appropriate column headings (labels) from the PivotTable Field List Box to the appropriate places in the pivot table.

Examples: Number of customers by:

✓ *REGION*
✓ *RENT VS. OWN*

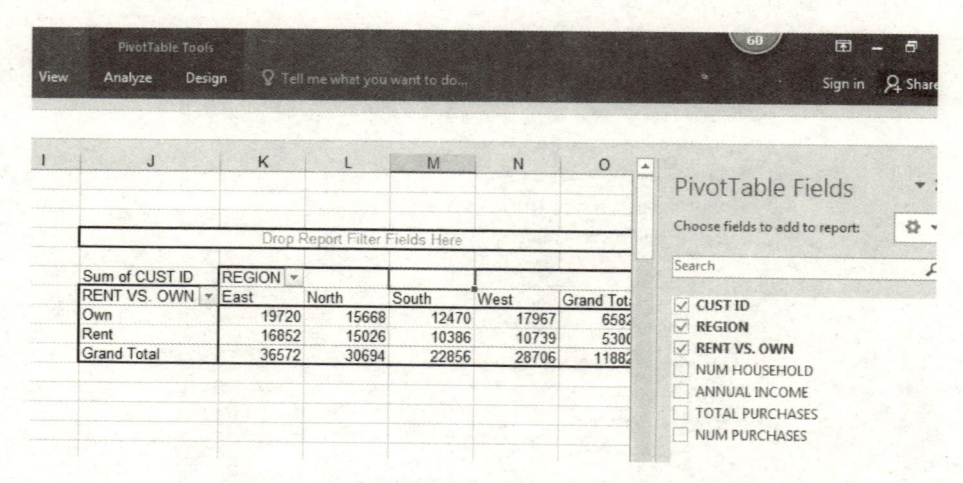

Figure 1.3.19   Drag and Drop Appropriate Column Headings (Labels)

The default aggregation for a pivot table is summing. To change it, select another aggregation by double-clicking on **Sum of CUST ID**, you will see the following box:

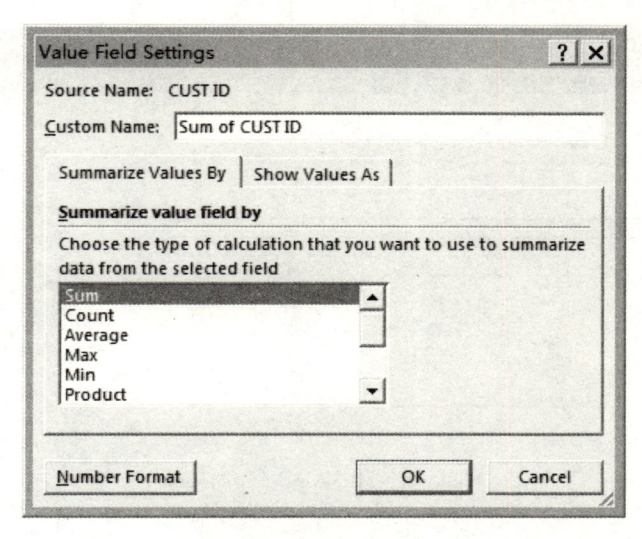

Figure 1.3.20 To Change into Another Aggregation

Pivot Tables can have multiple pieces of information in the body of the pivot table. Examples:
- ✓ Count of customers (already present)
- ✓ Total of purchases (new information)

Drag/drop *TOTAL PURCHASES* into a pivot table.

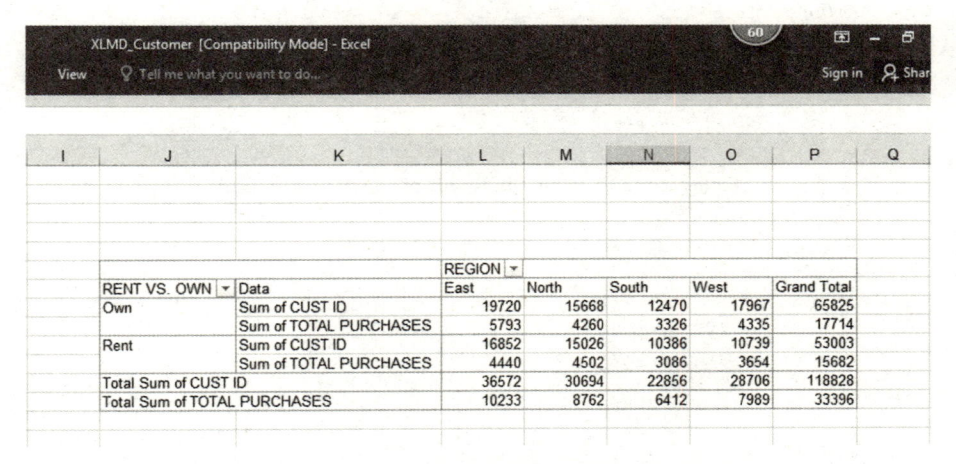

Figure 1.3.21 Pivot Tables of Multiple Pieces of Information

3D Pivot Table

Desired dimensions:
- ✓ *REGION*
- ✓ *RENT VS. OWN*
- ✓ *NUM HOUSEHOLD*

Drag/drop *NUM HOUSEHOLD* into "Drop Report Filter Fields Here" location.

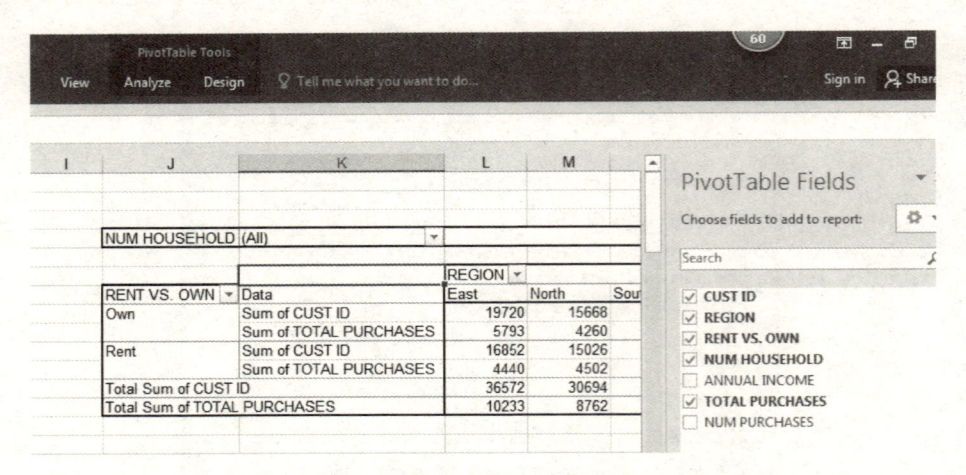

Figure 1.3.22　A 3D Pivot Table

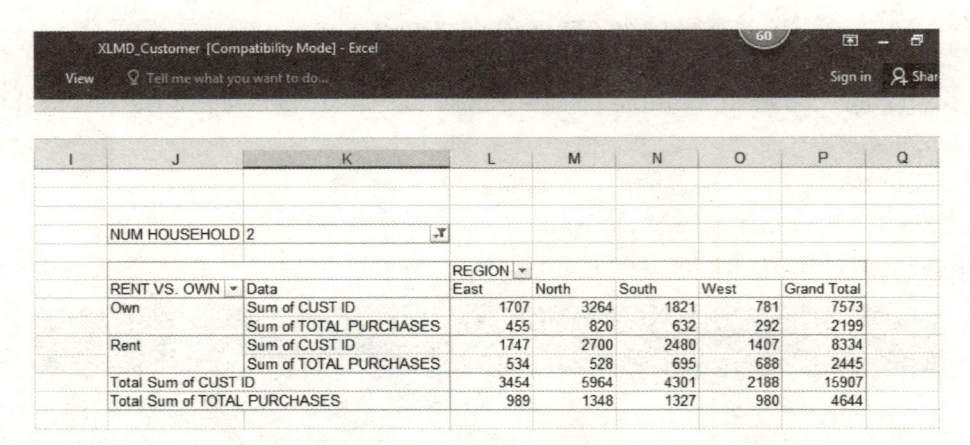

Figure 1.3.23　Show the Result of the 3D Pivot Table

Independent Experiment Guidance 4: E-Commerce Business Models

● **Introduction**

Nowadays, E-commerce is changing everything. **Electronic commerce (E-commerce)** is commerce, and it is accelerated and enhanced by IT, in particular by the Internet. We focus on building powerful relationships with customers, suppliers and partners. E-commerce business models are as follows:

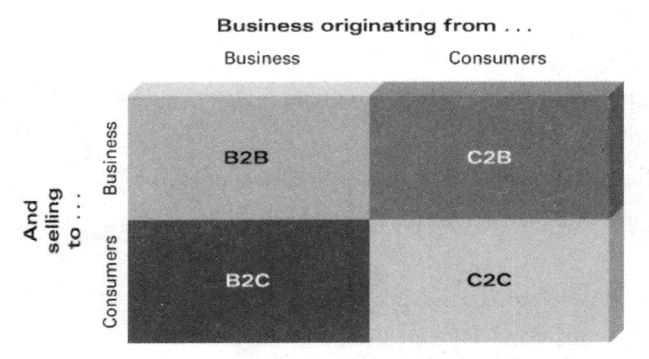

Figure 1.4.1 Common E-commerce Business Models

The most prominent are as follows:

1. *Business to Business* (*B2B*)— when a business sells products and services to customers who are primarily other businesses, such as **Alibaba.com**、慧聪(hc360).

2. *Business to Consumer* (*B2C*)— when a business sells products and services to individuals, such as Circuit City, Dangdang, Amazon etc.

● **E-Commerce Rules to Live by**

To be effective in E-commerce, you must:

1. Understand your business, products, services, and customers

For B2C:

(1) Greatly varying customer demographics, lifestyles, want and needs.

(2) Distinctions of products and services by convenience versus specialty products.

(3) E-commerce works best for commodities like digital products and services.

(4) Mass customization necessary in some instances.

For B2B:

(1) Distinctions of product and services by MRO versus direct materials.

(2) Demand aggregation is present.

(3) E-marketplaces connect buyers and sellers, including Horizontal (MRO materials mainly) and Vertical (direct materials mainly).

2. Find customers and establish relationships

For B2C：

(1) Design marketing mix, to drive potential customers to website.

(2) Register with search engines, online ads, viral marketing, and affiliate programs.

(3) Conversion rates measure success.

For B2B：

(1) Frequently occurring in an E-marketplace.

(2) Require establishing formal business relationship based on trust and continuity.

(3) Require IT system integration.

(4) Online negotiation for pricing, quality, specification and delivery timing.

3. Move money easily and securely

For B2C：

(1) Methods include credit cards, financial cybermediaries, electronic checks, EBPP, smart cards, and digital wallets.

(2) Pay for individual purchases, usually in small amounts.

(3) Each payment must be validated.

For B2B：

(1) Use EDI to facilitate ordering process.

(2) VANS can provide for EDI and financial EDI.

(3) Use financial EDI for payment of purchases.

4. B2C and B2B—security…

For both B2C and B2B：

(1) Overriding concern.

(2) Provided by the use of Encryption, SSLs, SET, and others.

◆2 Independent Experiment Report

Independent Experiment Report 1

Project Name   Identifying Hardware and Software
Laboratory   Unlimited
Affiliated Course   Introduction to Information Systems
Experiment Type   Design
Date

Class
Student No.
Name
Grading

Experiment Overview:

【Experiment Objectives and Requirements】
1. Familiar with computer components.
2. Identify hardware and software.

Requirements: Suppose you are a designer, graduate student or game player (choose one role), pick up a recent copy of your local newspaper or perhaps a computer magazine or on Internet and find a personal computer system for yourself. What is the price of the complete system? What hardware devices does it include? What software devices does it include? Identify all the various computer components and place them into suitable categories of information technology hardware and software.

【Experiment Principle】
1. Know hardware category and software category.
2. Hardware includes input device, output device, processing device, storage device, telecommunication device and connecting device.
3. Software includes application software and system software.

【Experiment Environment】(used hardware and software)
Internet condition, 1 PC/Person.

Experiment Content:

【Experiment Solution Design】

Your role	
The price of the complete system	

Hardware devices	Price	Category
...		

2 Independent Experiment Report

续表

Software devices	Price	Category
...		

【Summary】(your thinking or suggestions or gains in depth of comprehension)

Instructor comments:

Score:

Sign:
Date:

Independent Experiment Report 2

Project Name   Implementing a Database with Microsoft Access
Laboratory   Computer Lab
Affiliated Course   Introduction to Information Systems
Experiment Type   Integrated Experiment
Date

Class
Student No.
Name
Grading

2 Independent Experiment Report

Experiment Overview:

【Experiment Objectives and Requirements】
1. Identify the steps necessary to implement the structure of a relational database using the data definition language provided by microsoft Access.
2. Demonstrate how to use the data manipulation subsystem in access to enter and change information in a database and how to query that information.
3. Explain the use of the application generation subsystem in access to create reports and data entry screens.

【Experiment Principle】
Using Microsoft Access implement Solomon Enterprise Database.

【Experiment Environment】(used hardware and software)
1. Hardware: Desktop or laptop.
2. Software: Windows XP and Microsoft Access.

Experiment Content:

【Experiment Solution Design】
The steps of designing and implementing the correct structure of a relational database include:
1. Define entity classes and primary keys.
2. Define relationships among the entity classes.
3. Define information (fields) for each relation (the term relation is often used to refer to a file in the context of a database).
4. Use a data definition language to create your database.

【Experiment Procedure】(experiment steps, record, data and analysis)
1. Implementing the structure of the Solomon Enterprise Database.
2. Implementing the raw material relation structure.
3. Implementing the concrete type relation.
4. Implementing the bill of material relation.
5. Defining relationships within the Solomon Enterprise Database.
6. Entering information into the Solomon Enterprise Database.
7. Changing the structure of information in relations.
8. Creating a simple query using one relation.
9. Simple query with a condition (conditional query).
10. Creating an advanced query using more than one relation.
11. Generating a simple report.
12. Generating a report with grouping, sorting, and totals.
13. Creating a data input form.
14. Creating an account receivable report.

【Conclusion】(result)
1. The picture showing the relationships within the Solomon Enterprise Database.

2. The picture showing the advanced query using more than one relation.

3. The picture showing the report with grouping, sorting and totals.

4. The picture showing a data input form.

5. The picture showing an account receivable report.

【Summary】(your thinking or suggestions or gains in depth of comprehension)

Instructor comments:

Score:

Sign:
Date:

Independent Experiment Report 3

Project Name   Operating IT systems(DSS)

Laboratory   Unlimited

Affiliated Course   Introduction to Information Systems

Experiment Type   Verification

Date

Class

Student No.

Name

Grading

Experiment Overview:

【Experiment Objectives and Requirements】
Feel and operate various IT systems, compare and analyze the differences among them, and grasp them well.

Requirements: At present, feel and operate functions of Decision Support System according to experiment guidance, finish the tasks under experiment guidances step by step, paste the operation results into the part of experiment content.

【Experiment Principle】
1. Seven IT systems.
2. Definition, characteristics of each IT system.
3. Information processing tasks that each IT system is responsible for.

【Experiment Environment】(used hardware and software)
Windows operating system, personal computer, the demo base and files needed that professor provides.

Experiment Content:

【Experiment Solution Design】
1. Feeling what the decision support is.
2. Data processing and analysis : using filter, conditional formatting and pivot tables.

【Conclusion】(paste your operation results here)
1. The screen dump(print screen) of basic AutoFilter example (multiple columns).

2. The screen dump of custom AutoFilter example.

3. The screen dump of another custom AutoFilter example.

4. The screen dump of conditional formatting example.

5. The screen dump of 2D pivot table example.

6. The screen dump of 3D pivot table example.

2 Independent Experiment Report

【Summary】(your thinking or suggestions or gains in depth of comprehension)

Instructor comments:

Score:

Sign:
Date:

Independent Experiment Report 4

Project Name   Comparing Two Shopping Websites
Laboratory   Unlimited
Affiliated Course Introduction to Information Systems
Experiment Type Experiencing
Date

Class
Student No.
Name
Grading

2 Independent Experiment Report

Experiment Overview:

【Experiment Objectives and Requirements】
Experience shopping procedure by simulating method, grasp the characteristics and work procedures of electronic commerce, encourage students to do more looking, do more operating, and do more thinking, consolidate what the candidates learn in class and realize combination of theory and practice.

【Experiment Principle】
1. Electronic commerce business model.
2. Electronic commerce rules to live by.

【Experiment environment】(used hardware and software)
1. Internet connection.
2. Hardware: Desktop or laptop.
3. Software: Windows XP or other operation systems.
4. Internet Explorer or other browsers.

Experiment Content:

【Experiment Solution Design】
Recognize the characteristics of B2B(or B2C, or C2C) electronic commerce model by simulating shopping, show and summary the differences between domestic and foreign website.

【Experiment Procedure】(experiment steps, record, data and analysis)
1. Choose two shopping websites, one is Chinese website, the other is foreign website(Note: the two websites should belong to the same business model).
2. Simulate shopping, study or check the shopping flow, not necessarily pay bill successfully.
3. Pay attention to the same or different items between the two websites.
4. Tell your feelings and suggestions.

【Conclusion】(result)
1. The picture of domestic website you choose(logo).

2. The picture of foreign website you choose (logo).

3. Tell the differences of shopping procedures between the two websites (simple words).

4. Which shopping chain(flow) is more reasonable or comfortable? (simple words)

5. Suggestions for domestic or foreign website (simple words).

【Summary】(your thinking or suggestions or gains in depth of comprehension)

Instructor comments:

Score:

Sign:
Date:

第二部分 集成实验

1 集成实验指导

集成实验指导 1：保证输入数据的正确性

1. "输入掩码"技术

"输入掩码"控制用户向数据库中输入数据的方式。当希望以特定方式输入数据时，可以使用输入掩码。例如，数字掩码，即屏蔽非数字类型的字符的输入，换句话说，要求只能输入数字。

输入掩码包含三部分，所有这些部分都用分号";"隔开。

第一部分定义掩码字符串，由占位符和字面字符组成。

第二部分定义是否希望将掩码字符和任何数据一起存储到数据库中。若希望同时存储掩码和数据，则输入 0；若只希望存储数据，则输入 1。

第三部分定义用来指示数据位置的占位符。在默认情况下，Access 使用下划线（_）。若希望使用其他字符，则在掩码的第三部分输入该字符。例如，(999) 000－000；0；?（非规范写法，但系统会自动认为（ ）为字符，会为其自动加上""或者\）。

可输入掩码的数据包括类型、文本、日期/时间、数字和货币数据。

掩码使用列表如下：

0 代表数字 0～9；

9 代表数字或空格；

♯ 代表数字或空格；

? 代表字母 A～Z；

A 代表字母或数字。

下面以"产品类别表"为例，列示输入掩码的具体创建步骤：

(1) 对着"产品类别表"按鼠标右键，在弹出菜单中点击"设计视图"，选中"类别 ID"，点击下面的输入掩码对应编辑栏，如图 2.1.1 所示。

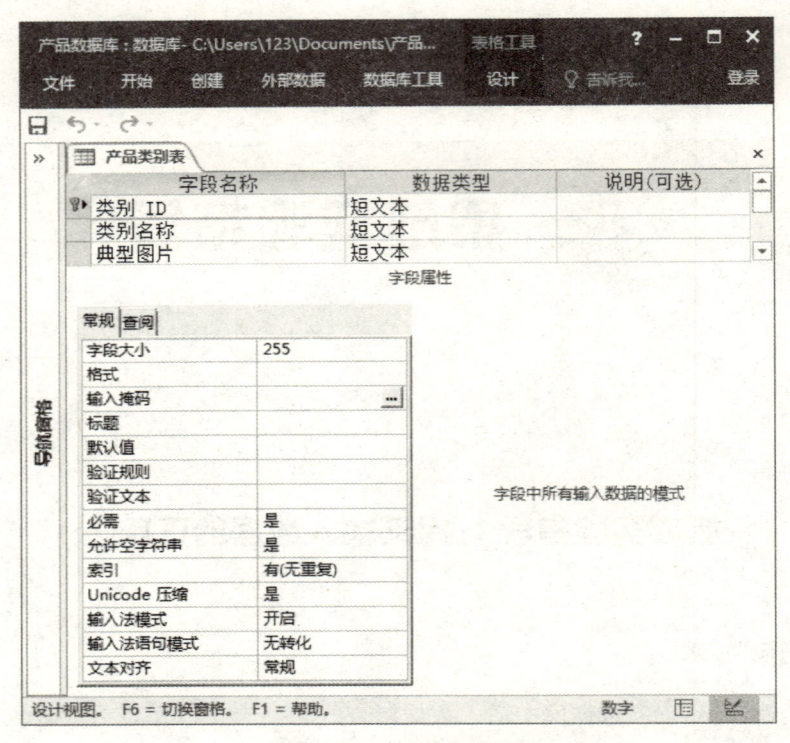

图 2.1.1 输入掩码编辑栏

(2)点击右侧省略号,出现如图 2.1.2 所示窗口。

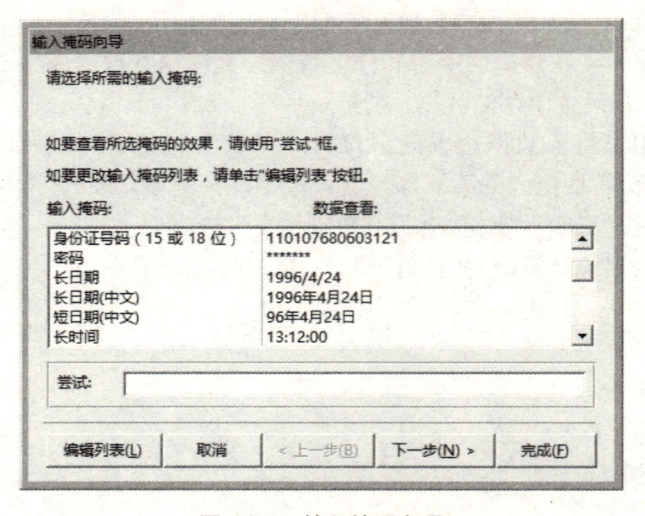

图 2.1.2 输入掩码向导

(3)如果事先没有保存表,会出现提示保存表的对话框。在保存表后出现如图 2.1.2 所示的输入掩码向导。选择"编辑列表(L)",出现如图 2.1.3 所示窗口。

1　集成实验指导

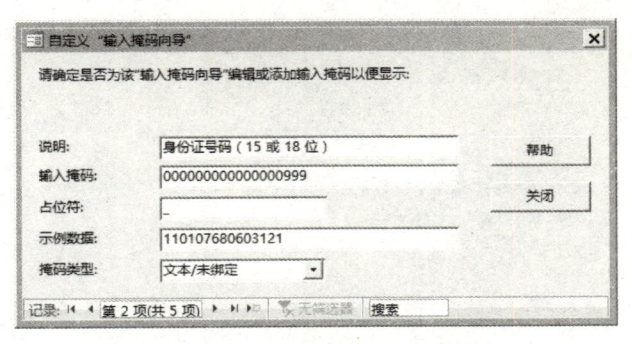

图 2.1.3　自定义"输入掩码向导"

(4)设计类别 ID 的输入掩码如图 2.1.4 所示。

图 2.1.4　设计输入掩码

(5)点击"关闭"按钮后,在列表中显示如图 2.1.5 所示窗口。

图 2.1.5　设计好的输入掩码

(6)点击"下一步(N)"按钮,选择占位符,可以自由选择占位符,如图 2.1.6 所示。

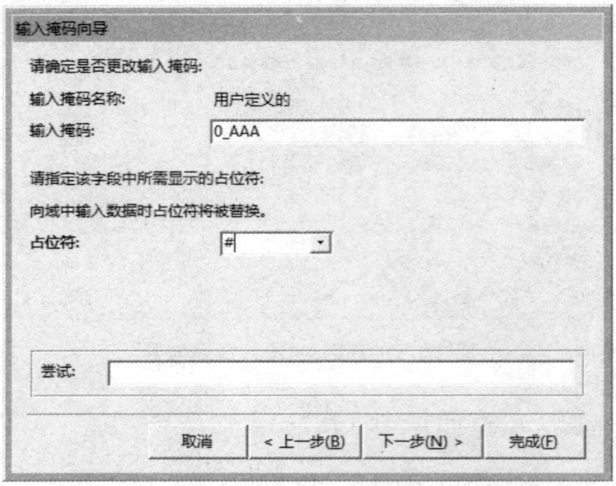

图 2.1.6　选择占位符

(7)点击"下一步(N)"按钮,选择保存数据的方式,如图 2.1.7 所示。

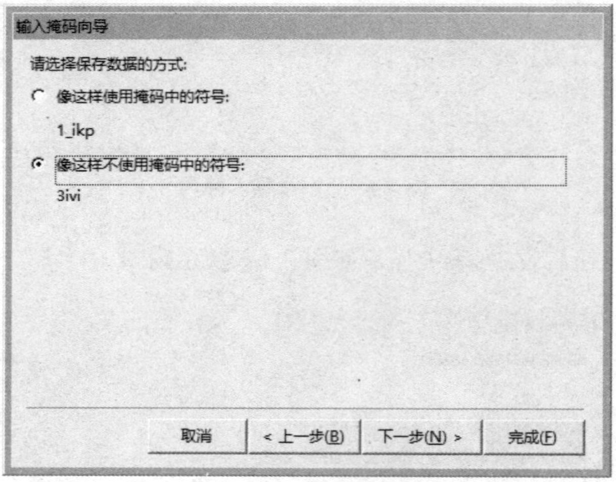

图 2.1.7　选择保存数据的方式

（8）点击"下一步(N)"按钮，出现提示确认页，如图 2.1.8 所示。

图 2.1.8　提示确认页

（9）点击"完成(F)"按钮，输入掩码创建成功，如图 2.1.9 所示。

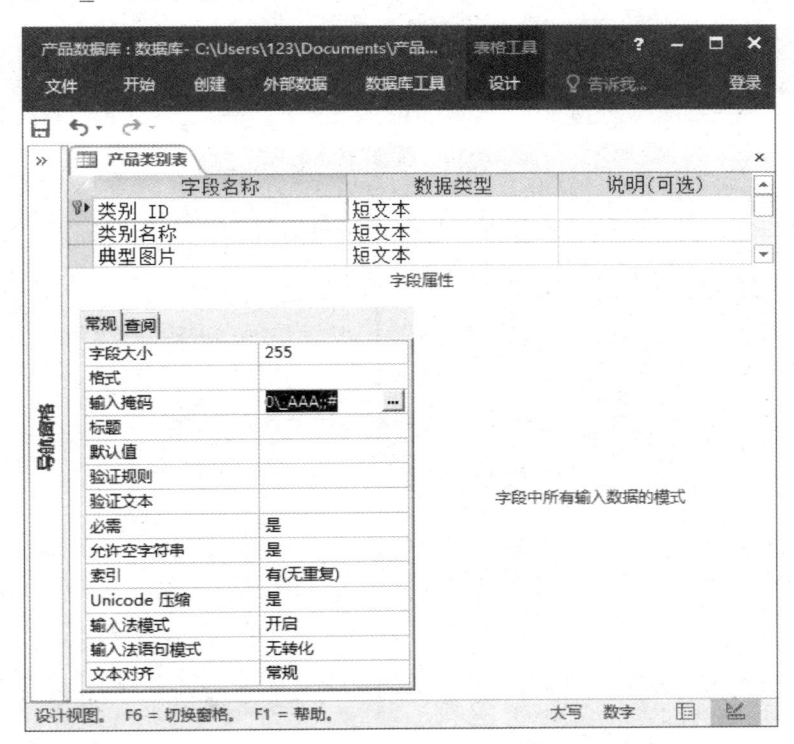

图 2.1.9　输入掩码创建成功

在之后的数据录入部分，它会起作用，控制数据录入合规与否。

2. "下拉菜单"技术

具体操作步骤如下：

(1)选中"产品类别表",按鼠标右键出现弹出菜单,点击"设计视图",进入表设计界面,在字段名称"类别名称"所对应的数据类型下拉菜单处选择"查阅向导…",如图 2.1.10 所示。

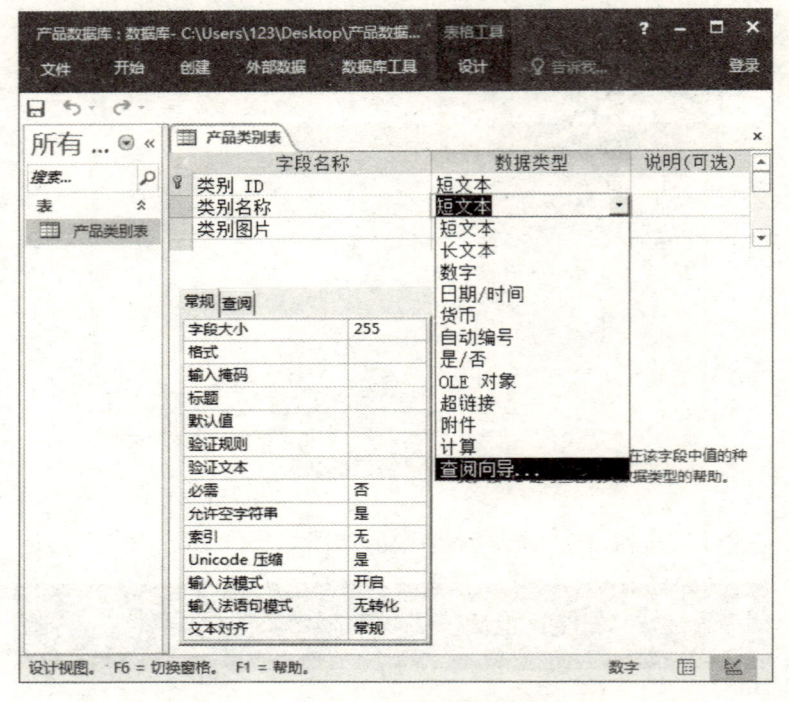

图 2.1.10　启动"查阅向导"

(2)点击"查阅向导…"后,出现如图 2.1.11 所示对话框。

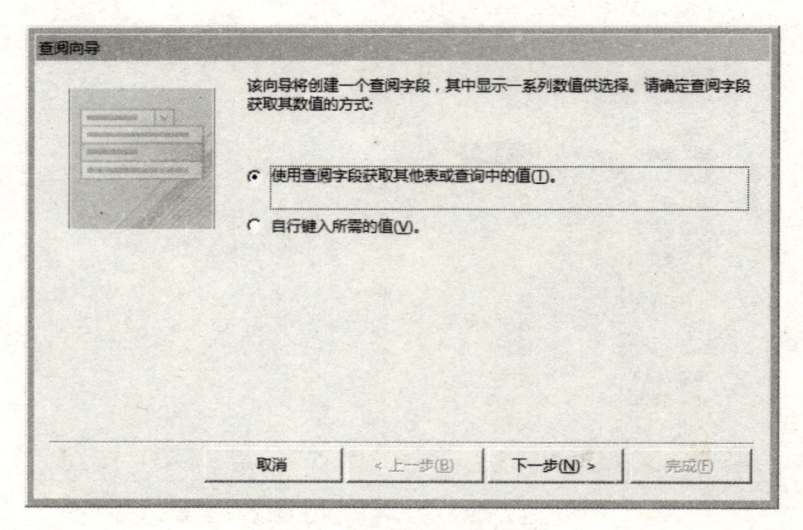

图 2.1.11　查阅向导对话框

(3)选择"自行键入所需的值(V)",点击"下一步(N)"按钮,在出现的窗体中录入列的信息,即类别名称"手机导航仪、电脑设备、办公设备、数码产品、电视家庭影音、厨卫器具"六种,如图 2.1.12 所示。

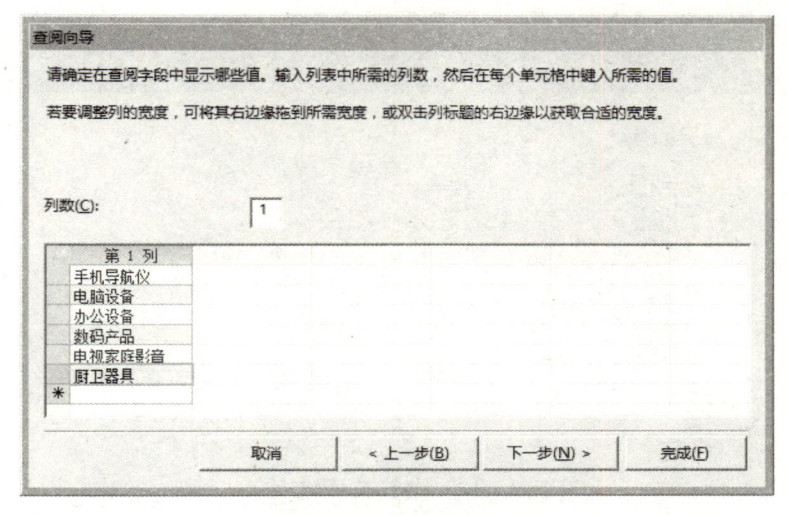

图 2.1.12　录入列信息

(4) 点击"下一步(N)"按钮,出现如图 2.1.13 所示窗口。

图 2.1.13　指定标签

(5) 点击"完成(F)"按钮,结束定义,回到表设计视图,点击下面的"查阅"菜单,可见如图 2.1.14 所示窗口。若出现该窗口,则证明关于类别名称的下拉菜单设置成功,日后数据录入时可以在下拉菜单中选择。

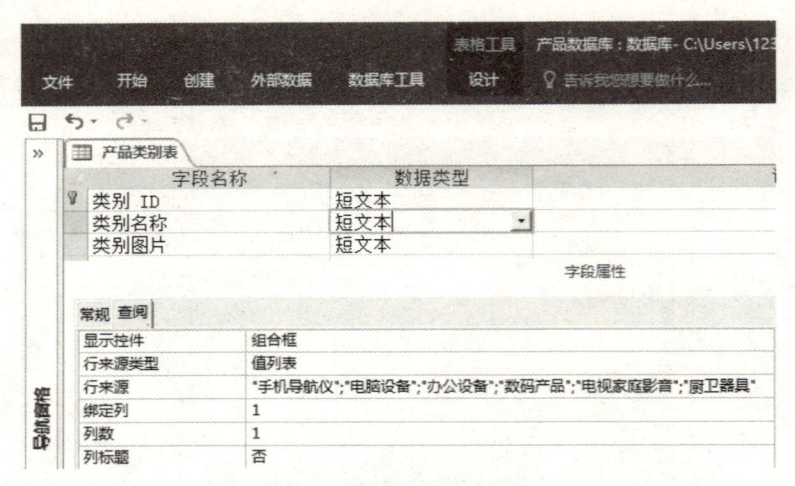

图 2.1.14 "查阅菜单"可见项

3. 对象连接与嵌入类型设置

具体操作步骤如下：

(1)选中"产品类别表"，进入表设计界面，在字段名称"类别图片"所对应的数据类型下拉菜单处选择"OLE 对象"，如图 2.1.15 所示。

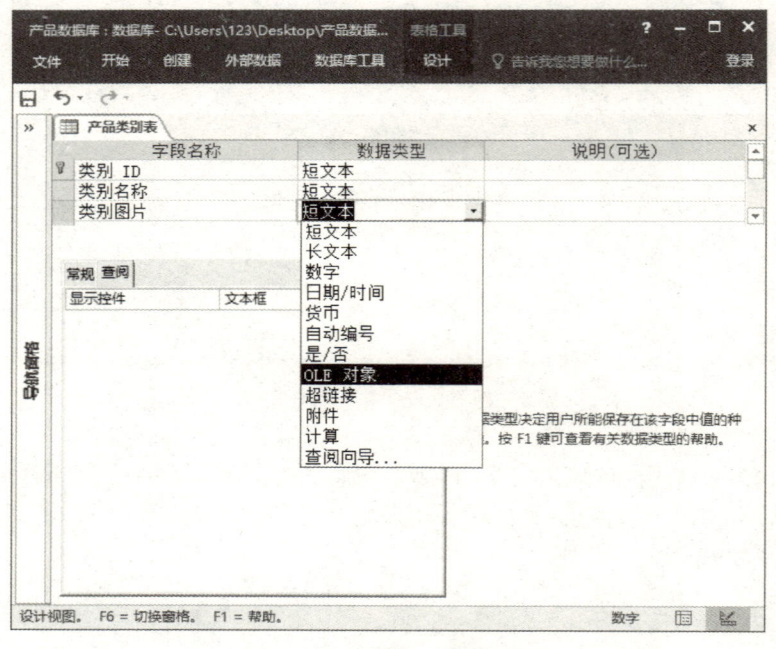

图 2.1.15 启动 OLE 对象

(2)若设置成功，则出现如图 2.1.16 所示界面。
以后可以使用其嵌入图片。

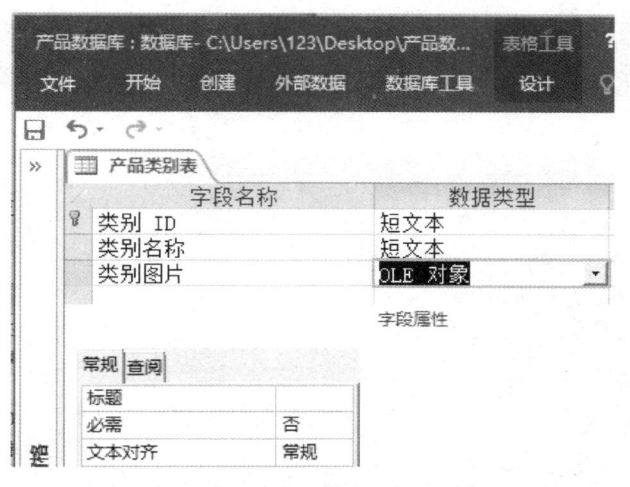

图 2.1.16　设置成功 OLE 对象

4. 数据从 Excel 导入 Access 数据库

具体操作步骤如下：
(1)点击"外部数据"菜单，选中 Excel 按键，如图 2.1.17 所示。

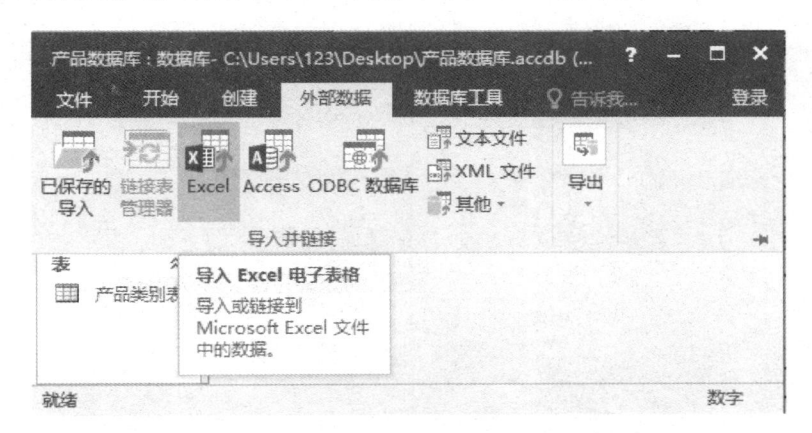

图 2.1.17　找到"导入"菜单项

(2)点击"导入 Excel 电子表格"，出现如图 2.18 所示界面，选择要导入的 Excel 表。注意指定数据在当前数据库中的存储方式和存储位置。

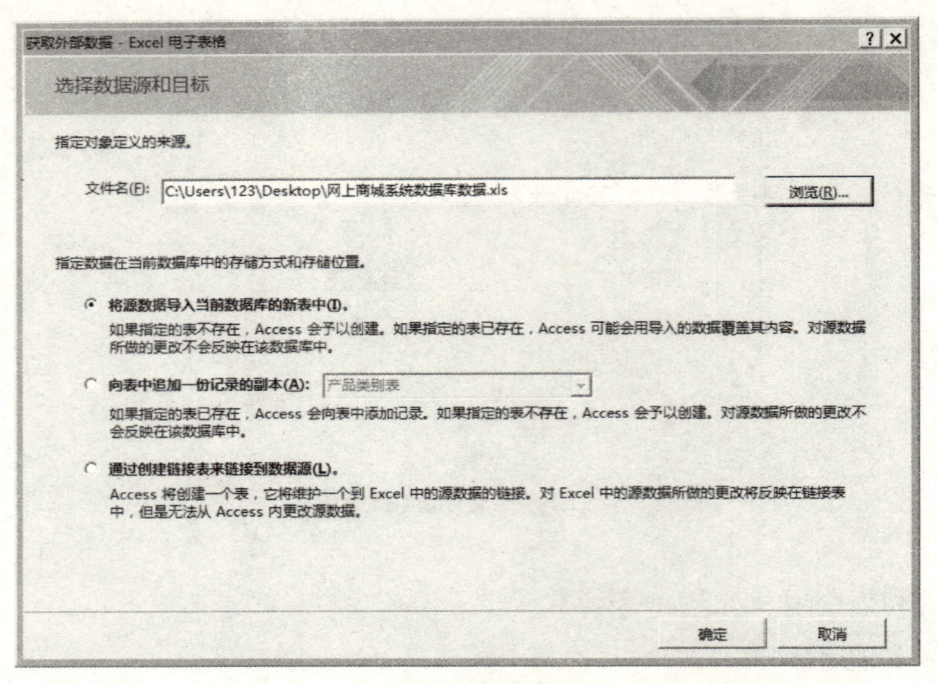

图 2.1.18　导入对话框

(3)点击"确定"按钮,出现如图 2.1.19 所示界面,选择要导入的表"tb_Class"。

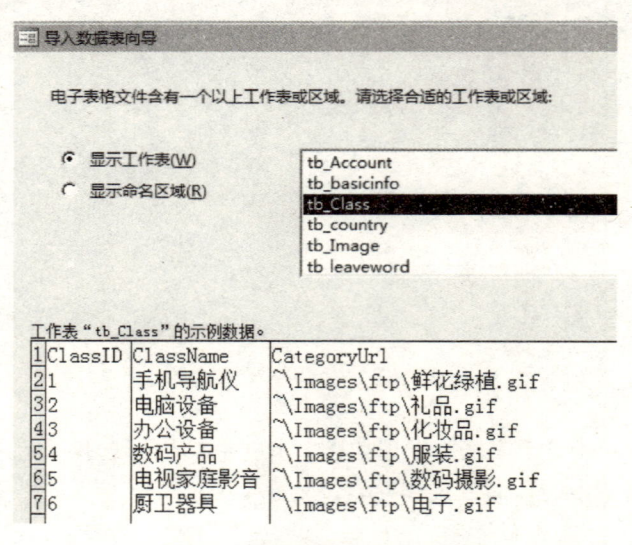

图 2.1.19　选择要导入的 Excel 表

(4)点击"下一步(N)"按钮,出现如图 2.1.20 所示界面。
(5)接着点击"下一步(N)"按钮,可以调整、修改字段信息,如图 2.1.21 所示。
(6)继续点击"下一步(N)"按钮,确定主键,如图 2.1.22 所示。

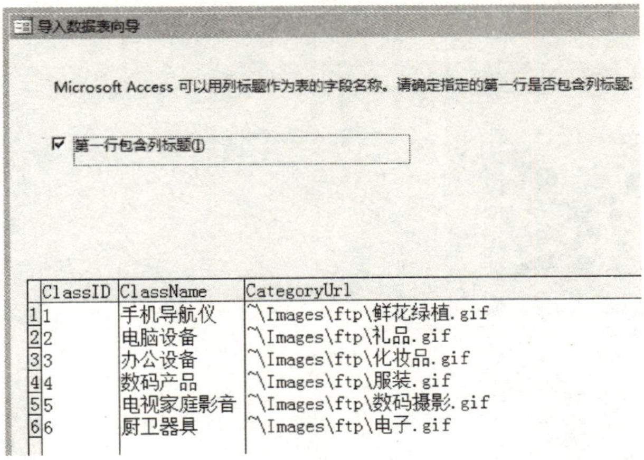

图 2.1.20　确定字段名称

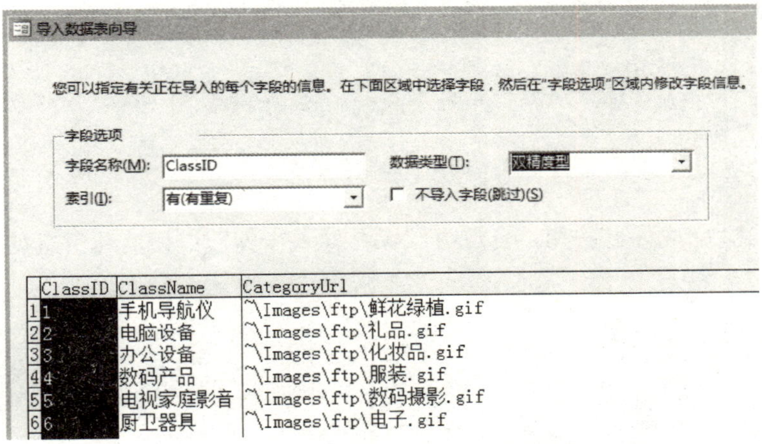

图 2.1.21　必要的字段信息更改

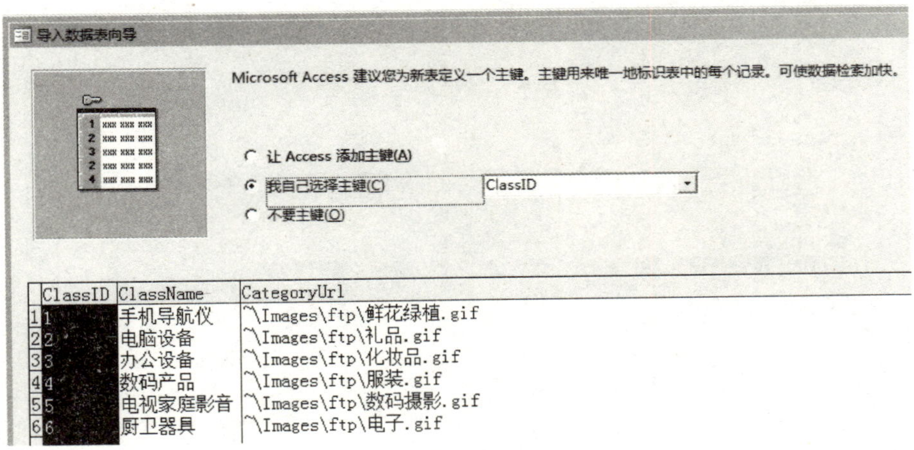

图 2.1.22　确定主键

(7)点击"下一步(N)"按钮,给表命名,如图 2.1.23 所示。

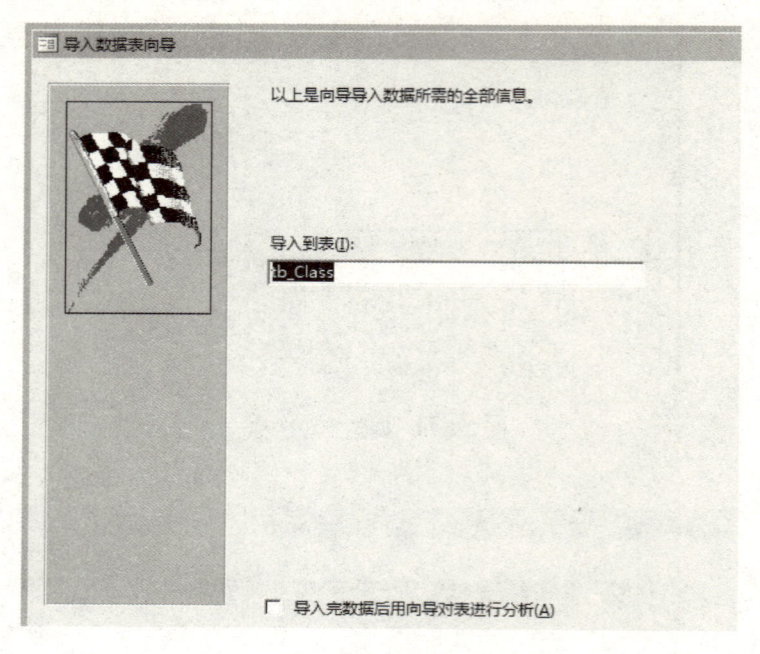

图 2.1.23　命名表

(8)最后点击"完成(F)"按钮,可以选择"保存导入步骤",以便简化后继使用,如图 2.1.24 所示。

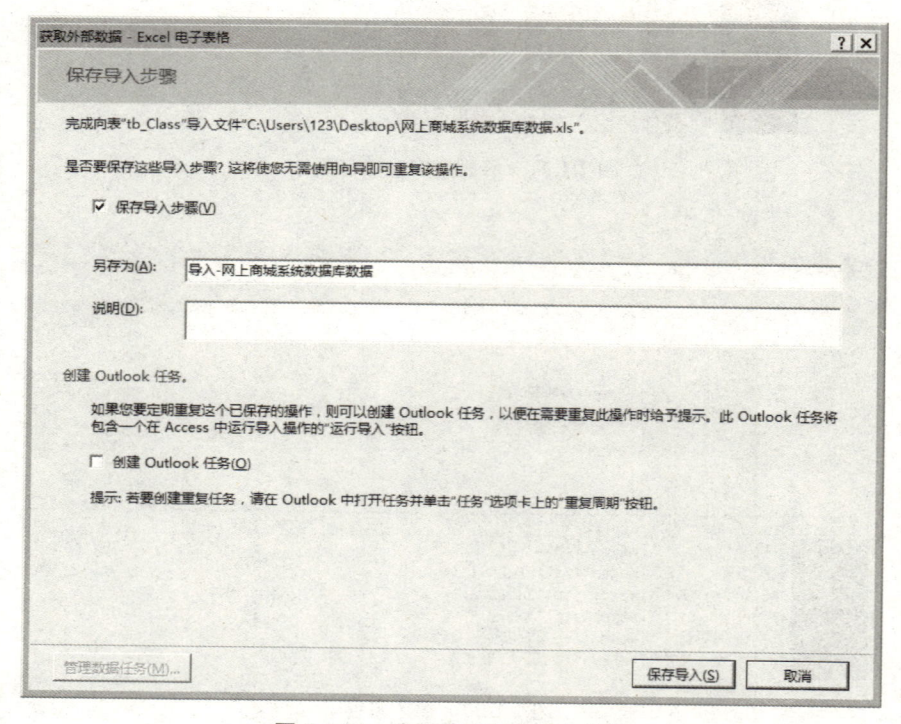

图 2.1.24　确认是否保存导入步骤

(9)表导入成功,如图 2.1.25 所示。

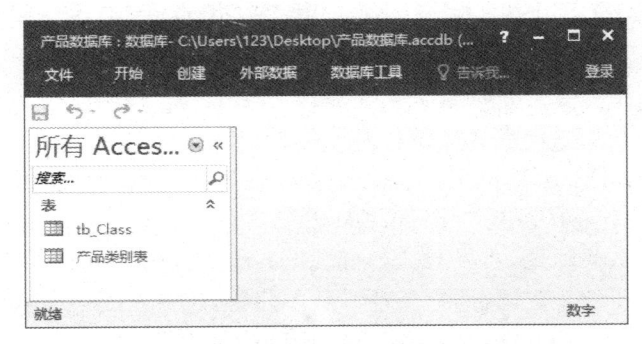

图 2.1.25　表导入成功

集成实验指导 2：网上商城的销售决策分析

1. 建立 ODBC 数据源

在利用 Microsoft Query 对网上商城进行数据查询之前，必须先建立一个用于连接该数据库的 ODBC 数据源"wssc"。基于 Excel 2016 的具体步骤如下：

步骤 1：利用 Microsoft Excel 的导入外部数据的功能，启动 Microsoft Query 应用程序。

创建一个空白的 Excel 文档，选中任意一个单元格，选择 Excel 菜单中的"数据"→"自其他来源"→"来自 Microsoft Query"，如图 2.2.1 所示。

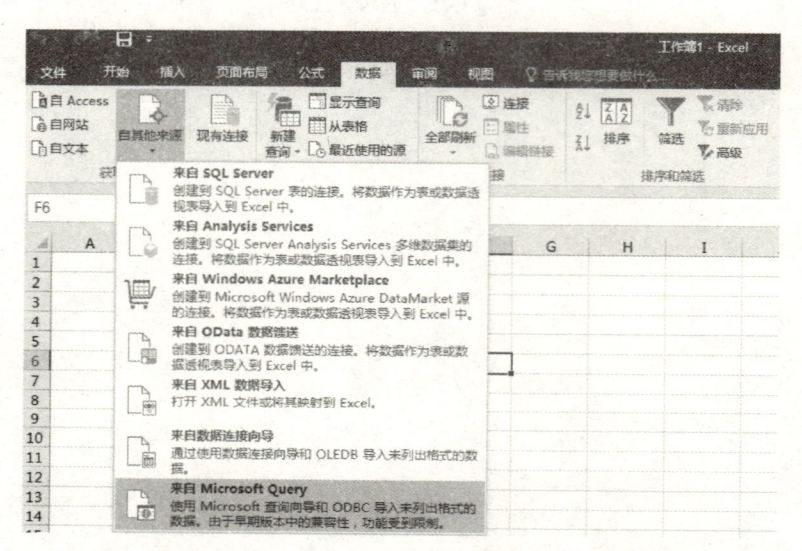

图 2.2.1　启动 Microsoft Excel 的导入外部数据功能

步骤 2：进入"选择数据源"对话框。

在新出现的如图 2.2.2 所示的"选择数据源"对话框内，选择"数据库"选项卡中的"〈新数据源〉"，再单击"确定"按钮，出现"创建新数据源"对话框，如图 2.2.3 所示。

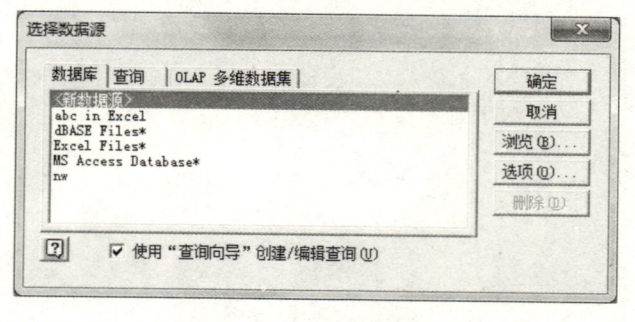

图 2.2.2　选择数据源窗口

1 集成实验指导

步骤 3:输入数据源名称。

在"创建新数据源"对话框的"请输入数据源名称:"项中输入要定义的数据源的名称("wssc"),如图 2.2.3 所示。

图 2.2.3 "创建新数据源"对话框

步骤 4:选择数据库驱动程序。

在"创建新数据源"对话框的"为您要访问的数据库类型选定一个驱动程序:"下拉列表框中选择与"网上商城系统数据库数据.xls"相匹配的驱动程序,即"Microsoft Excel Driver (*.xls,*.xlsx.*.xlsm,*.xlsb)",如图 2.2.4 所示。

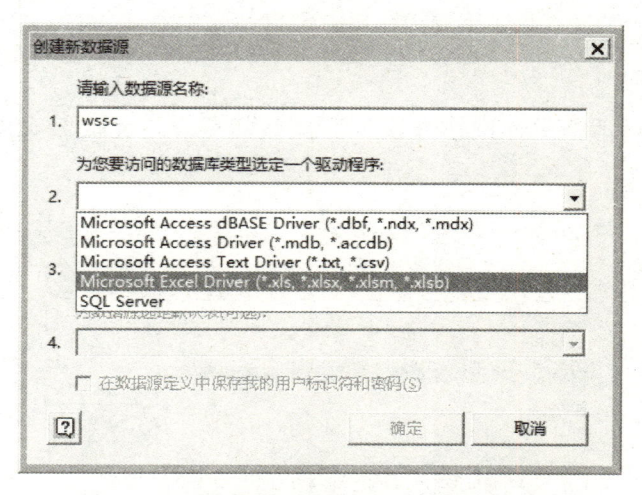

图 2.2.4 创建数据源对话框——选择驱动程序

步骤 5:定义数据库连接信息,即选择数据源所要引用的数据库"网上商城系统数据库数据.xls"。

单击"创建新数据源"对话框中的"连接(C)…"按钮,出现如图 2.2.5 所示的"ODBC Microsoft Excel 安装"对话框。

图 2.2.5 "ODBC Microsoft Access 安装"对话框

单击其中的"选择工作簿(S)…"按钮,出现如图 2.2.6 所示的"选择工作簿"对话框。选择"网上商城系统数据库数据.xls"数据库后,单击"确定"按钮。

图 2.2.6 "选择工作簿"对话框

在随后出现的对话框中连续按 2 次"确定"按钮后即可完成"wssc"数据源的定义,如图 2.2.7 所示。

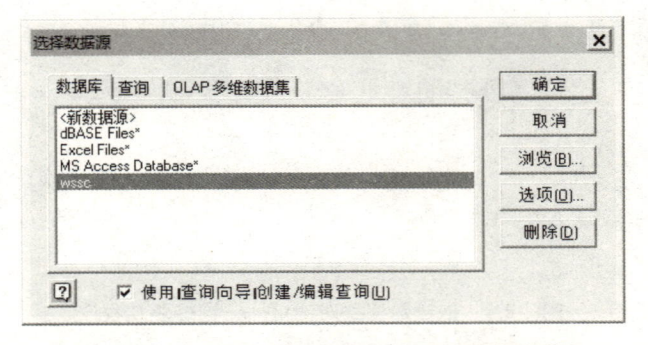

图 2.2.7 创建了数据源后的"选择数据源"对话框

2. 查询 2010 年 1 月～2011 年 10 月的销售数据

2010 年 1 月～2011 年 10 月的销售数据保存在 tb_Order 表和 tb_OrderItem 表中。查询步骤如下:

步骤 1:选择"wssc"数据源,进入"查询设计"窗口。

1　集成实验指导

在图 2.2.8 所示的"选择数据源"对话框中,选中"wssc"数据源,单击"确定"按钮,单击"使用'查询向导'创建/编辑查询(U)"项前面的复选框,使其处于未选中状态,再单击"确定"按钮,便可出现"查询设计"窗口及"添加表"对话框,如图 2.2.9 所示。

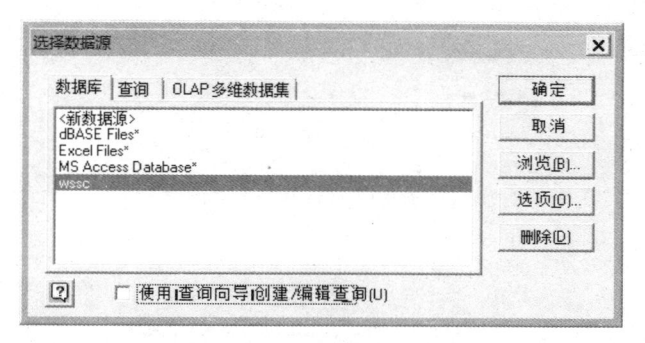

图 2.2.8　"选择数据源"对话框

步骤 2:选择查询中需要使用的表。

在"添加表"对话框的"表(I):"列表中,选择查询中将使用的表"tb_Order",单击"添加(A)"按钮,即将该表添加到"查询设计"窗口的"表"窗格中,如图 2.2.9 所示;选择查询中将使用的"tb_OrderItem"表,单击"添加"按钮,就可以将该表添加到"查询设计"窗口的"表"窗格中,如图 2.2.10 所示。单击"添加表"对话框的"关闭(C)"按钮,进入"查询设计"窗口。

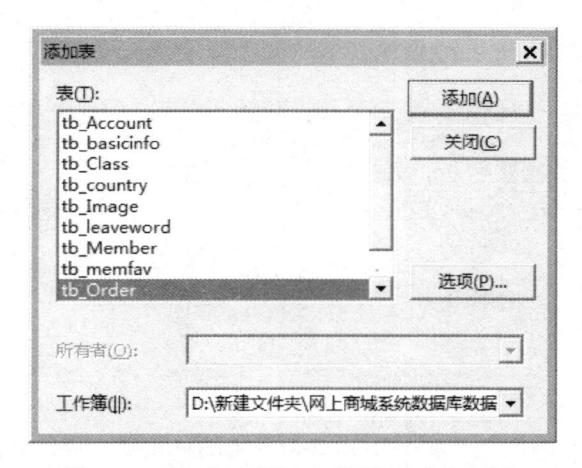

图 2.2.9　"查询设计"窗口及"添加表"对话框

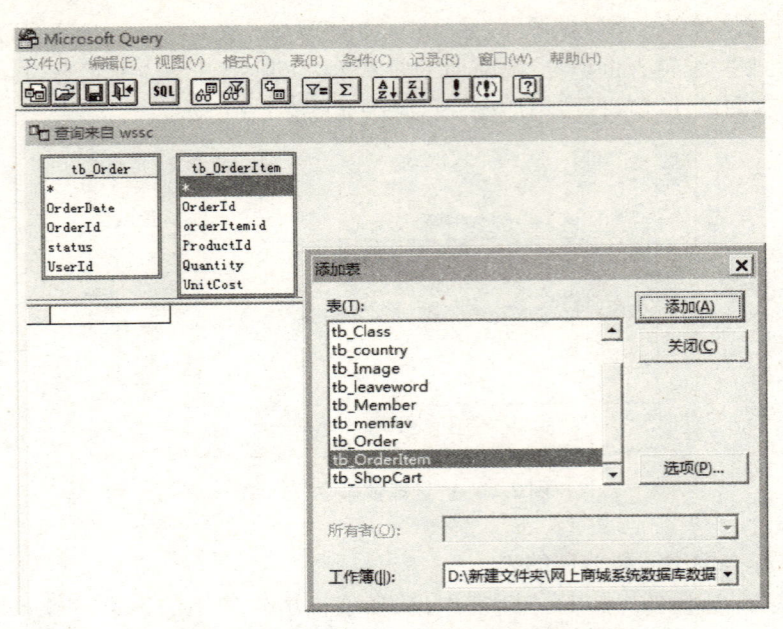

图 2.2.10　添加 tb_Order 和 tb_OrderItem 表

步骤 3：创建两个表之间的联系。

选中"tb_Order"表中的"OrderId"字段，拖动到"tb_OrderItem"表中的"OrderId"字段上方，松开鼠标左键，结果如图 2.2.11 所示。

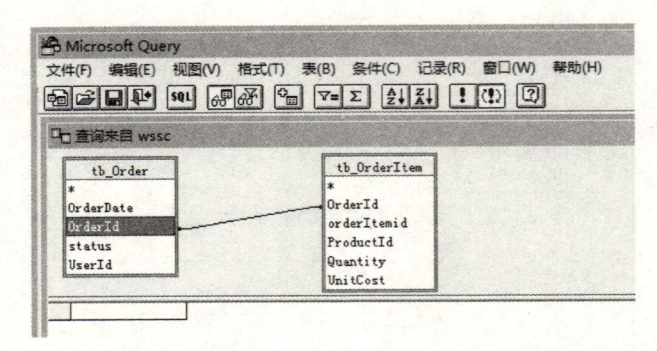

图 2.2.11　创建 tb_Order 表和 tb_OrderItem 表之间的联系

步骤 4：选择要查询的字段。

在"查询设计"窗口的"表"窗格中，分别双击"tb_Order"表中需要查询的"OrderDate"以及"tb_OrderItem"表中的"UnitCost"字段，查询结果如图 2.2.12 所示。

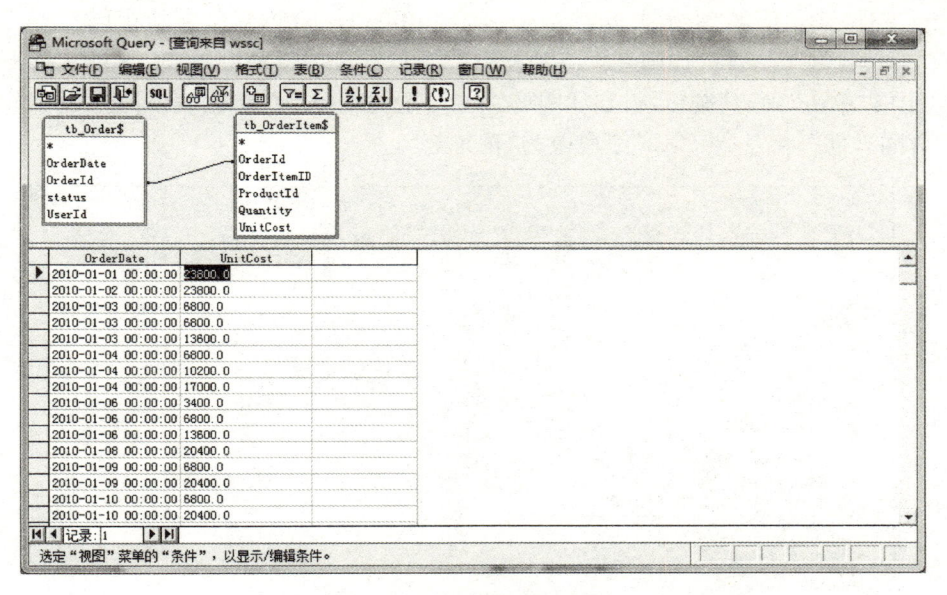

图 2.2.12 "查询设计"窗口

步骤 5：添加"条件"窗格，设置查询条件。

单击"视图"菜单中的"条件"命令，使"条件"项前面出现"√"，便可以在"查询设计"窗口中添加"条件"窗格。在"条件"窗格的"条件字段："行的第一列中选择"OrderDate"，并在下一行中输入"＞＝2010/1/1"后回车；在第二列中选择"OrderDate"，并在下一行中输入"＜＝2011/10/31"后回车，如图 2.2.13 所示，即可在"查询结果"窗格中显示 2010 年 1 月～2011 年 10 月的销售数据。

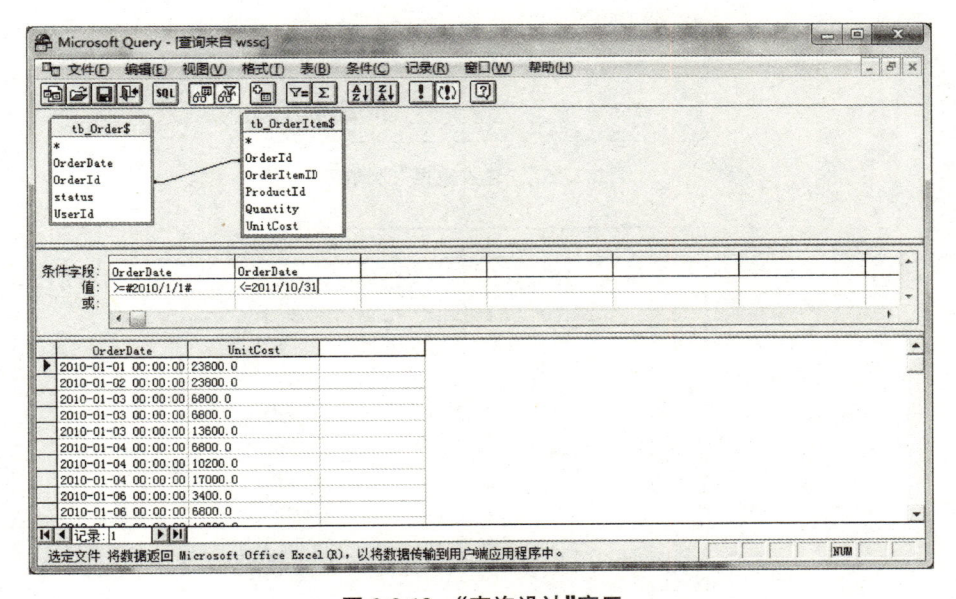

图 2.2.13 "查询设计"窗口

步骤 6：将数据返回 Excel。

单击"文件"菜单中的"将数据返回 Microsoft Office Excel(R)"命令,如图 2.2.14 所示,在 Excel 的"导入数据"对话框(如图 2.2.15 所示)中,数据的放置位置设为"现有工作表(E):",单击 A1 单元格,单击"确定"按钮,得到如图 2.2.16 所示的 Excel 数据列表,并将"OrderDate"字段改为"订购日期",将"UnitCost"字段改为"销售额"。

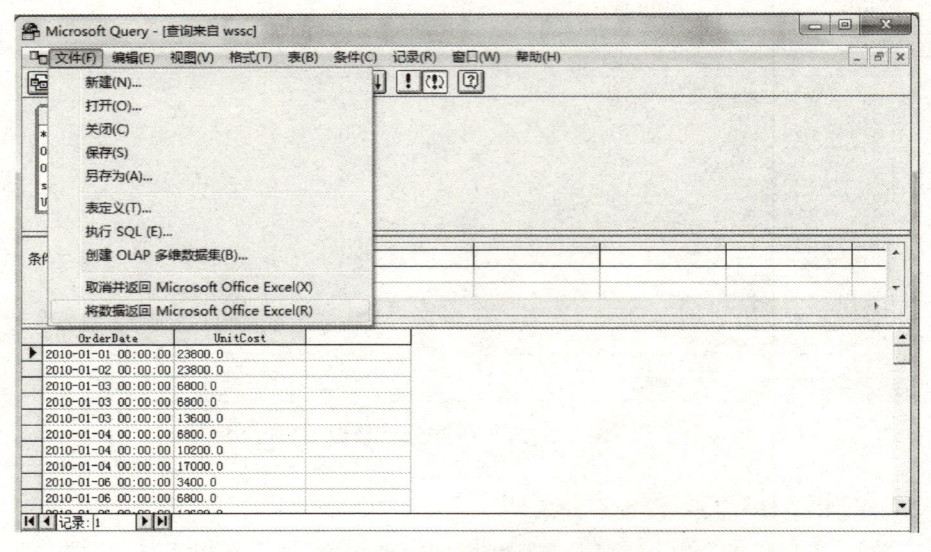

图 2.2.14　将数据返回 Excel

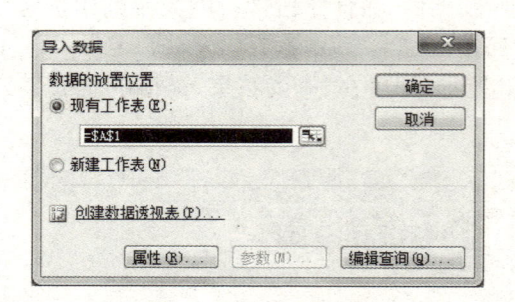

图 2.2.15　"导入数据"对话框

图 2.2.16　查询至 Excel 数据列表

3. 制作数据透视表,按月汇总销售数据

鉴于数据透视表的重要性,前面的独立实验 3 基于 EXCEL 2016 演示了数据透视表的操作,此处及下节基于 EXCEL 2000 演示,以供有不同需求的读者参考。需要 EXCEL 2016 数据透视表操作演示的,参见前面的独立实验 3。

利用数据透视表,按月汇总销售额的步骤如下:

步骤 1:创建数据透视表框架。

将光标停留在单元格 A1:B861 中的任意单元格,选择"数据"菜单中的"数据透视表和数据透视图"命令,选择数据源类型为"Microsoft Office Excel 数据列表或数据库(M)",所需创建的报表类型为"数据透视表",单击"下一步(N)"按钮,选择区域为 A1:B861,单击"下一步(N)"按钮,设定数据透视表位置为"新建工作表(N)",单击"完成(F)"按钮,如图 2.2.17~图 2.2.19 所示。

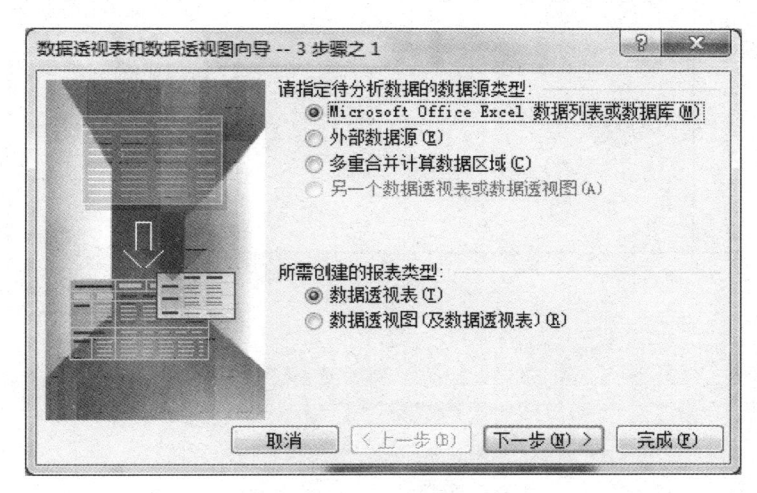

图 2.2.17 指定数据源类型

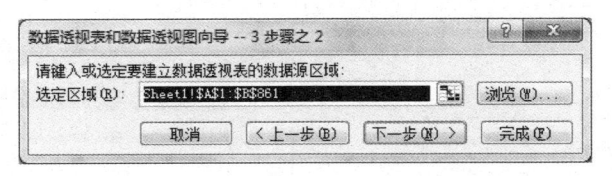

图 2.2.18 选定数据源区域

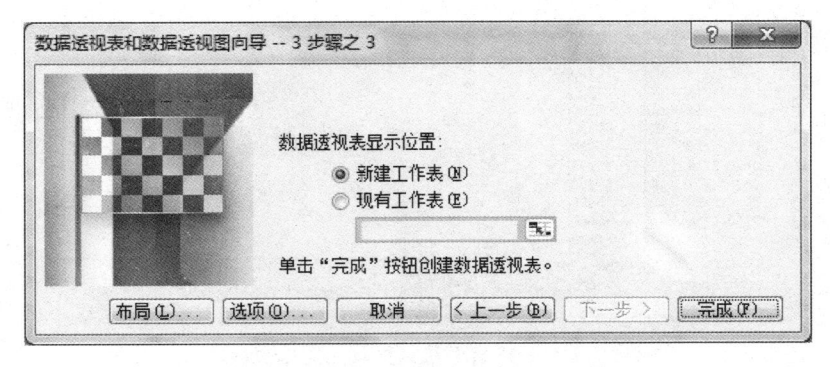

图 2.2.19 选定数据透视表显示位置

步骤 2：按订购日期汇总销售额。

在步骤 1 创建的数据透视表框架中，除了可以看到透视表框架以外，还出现了"数据透视表字段列表"框和"数据透视表"浮动工具栏。选中"数据透视表字段列表"框中的"订购日期"字段，将其拖动到数据透视表框架中的"将行字段拖至此处"，选中"数据透视表字段列表"框中的"销售额"字段，将其拖动到数据透视表框架中的"请将数据项拖至此处"（如图 2.2.20 所示），得到如图 2.2.21 所示的数据透视表，该透视表反映销售额已经按日汇总。

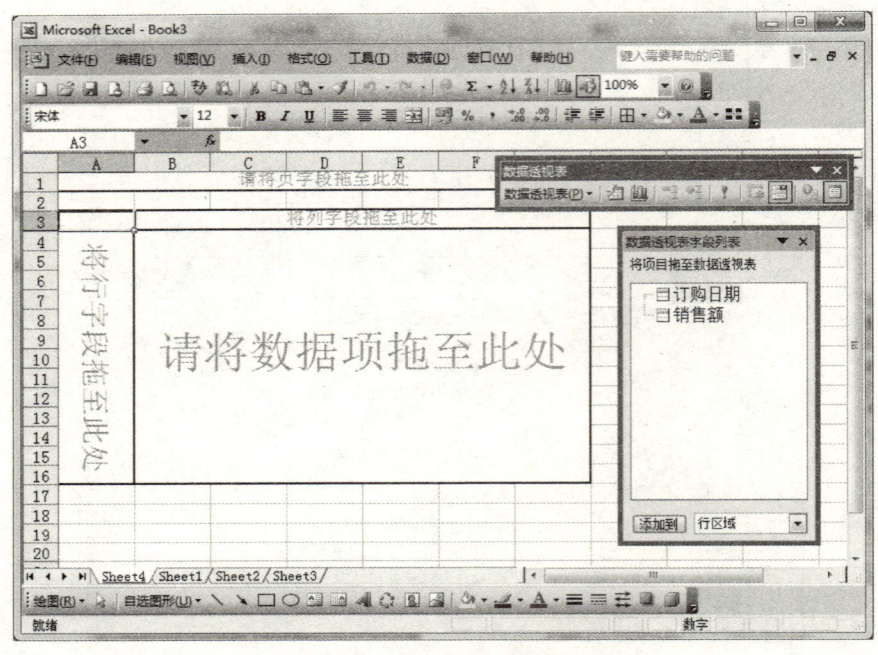

图 2.2.20　数据透视表框架

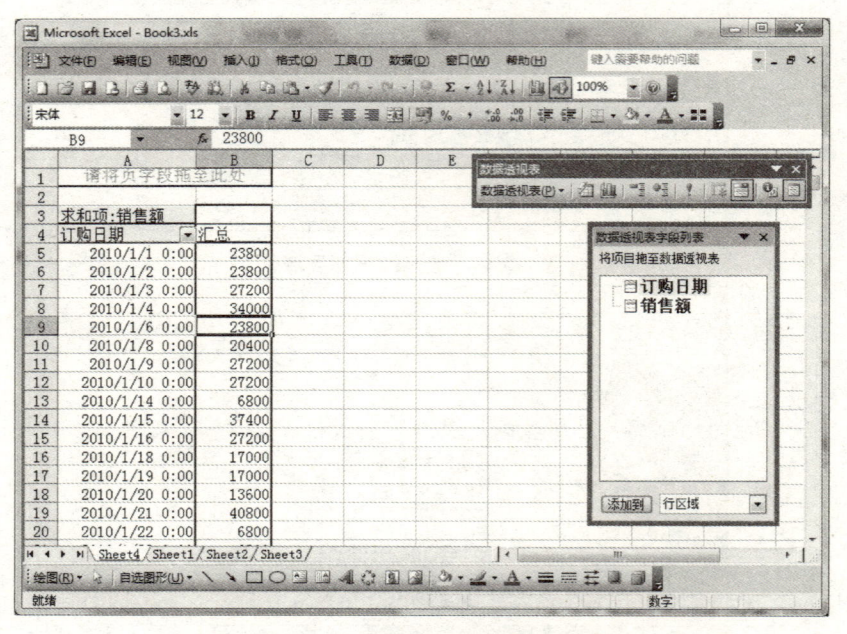

图 2.2.21　按日汇总销售额的数据透视表

步骤 3：按照订购年月组合订购日期。

选择"订购日期"所在的单元格 A4（或者单元格 A5：A478 中的任意单元格），右键单击鼠标，在弹出的快捷菜单中选择"组及显示明细数据/组合"命令，随后出现如图 2.2.22 所示的组合框，因为被组合的字段类型为日期型，Excel 允许按照"分""小时""日""月""季"和"年"等为组合依据组合数据。选择"月"和"年"作为组合依据，单击"确定"按钮，得到如图 2.2.23 所示的数据透视表。

图 2.2.22　分组对话框

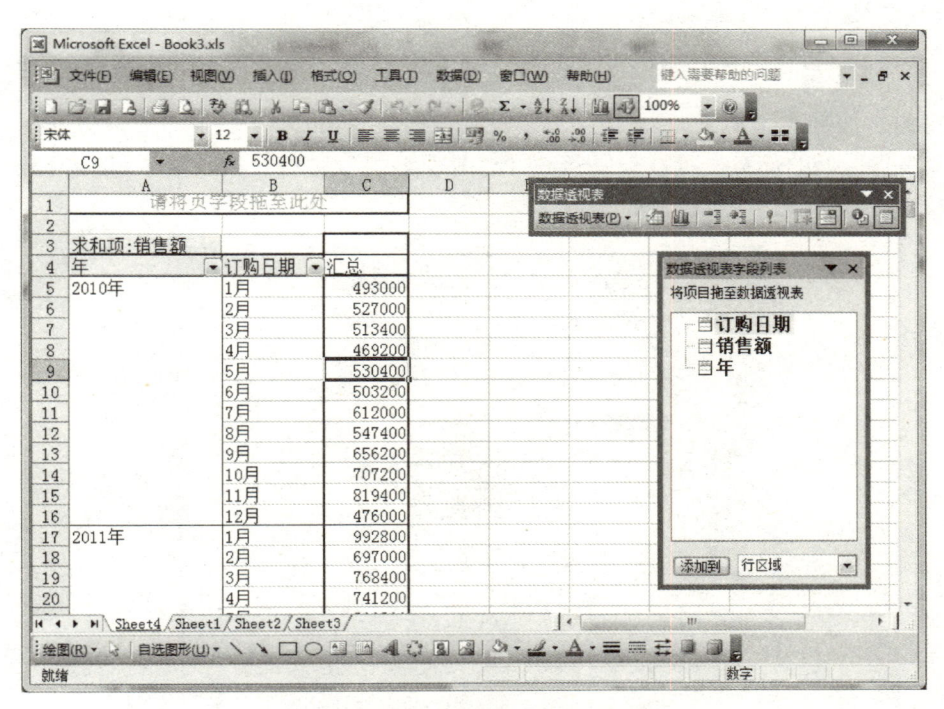

图 2.2.23　按年月汇总的数据透视表

4. 绘制数据透视图，预测未来销售额

步骤 1：绘制柱形数据透视图。

光标停留在数据透视表的任意一个单元格，选择菜单"插入"→"图表"，得到柱形数据透视图（如图 2.2.24 所示）。

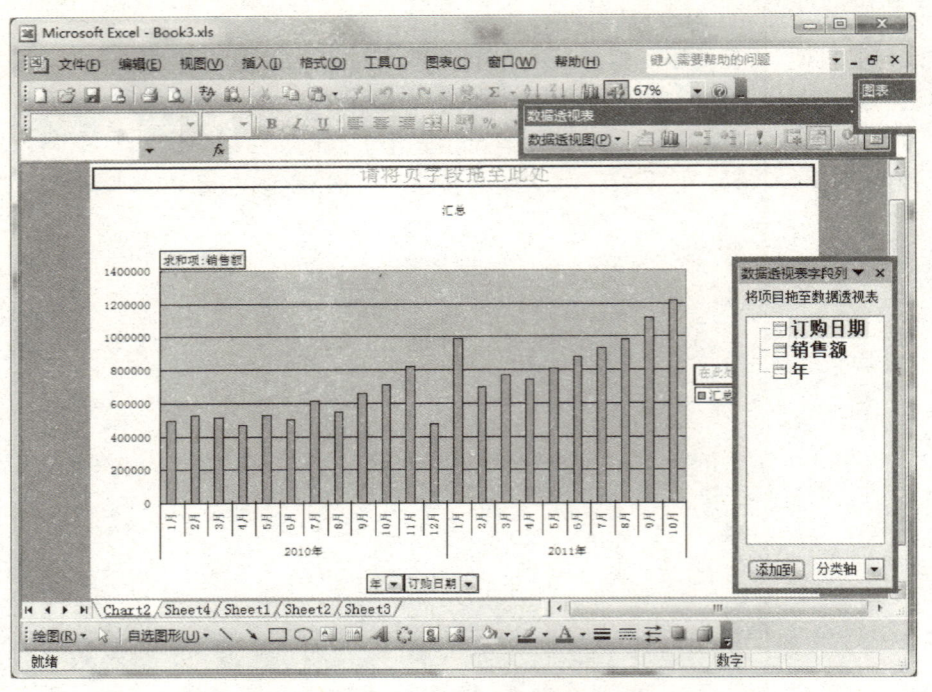

图 2.2.24　柱形数据透视图

步骤 2：修改图表类型。

在图表空白处的任意位置右击鼠标，选择"图表类型"，如图 2.2.25 所示，设定图表类型为折线图，就得到折线形数据透视图，如图 2.2.26 所示。

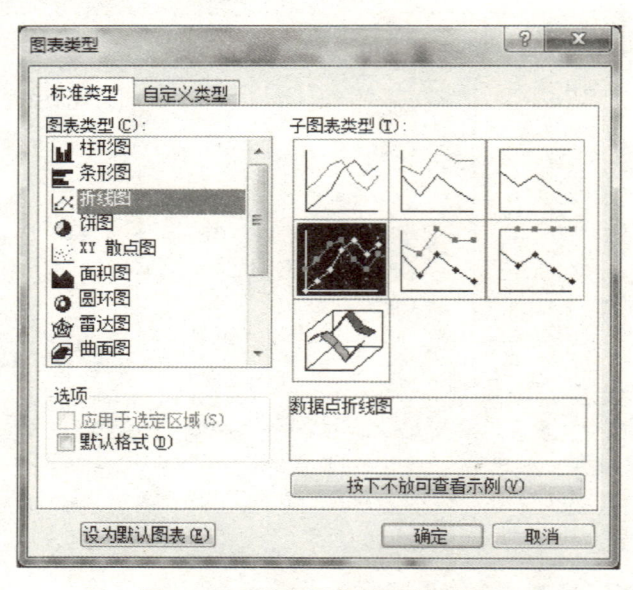

图 2.2.25　设定图表类型为折线图

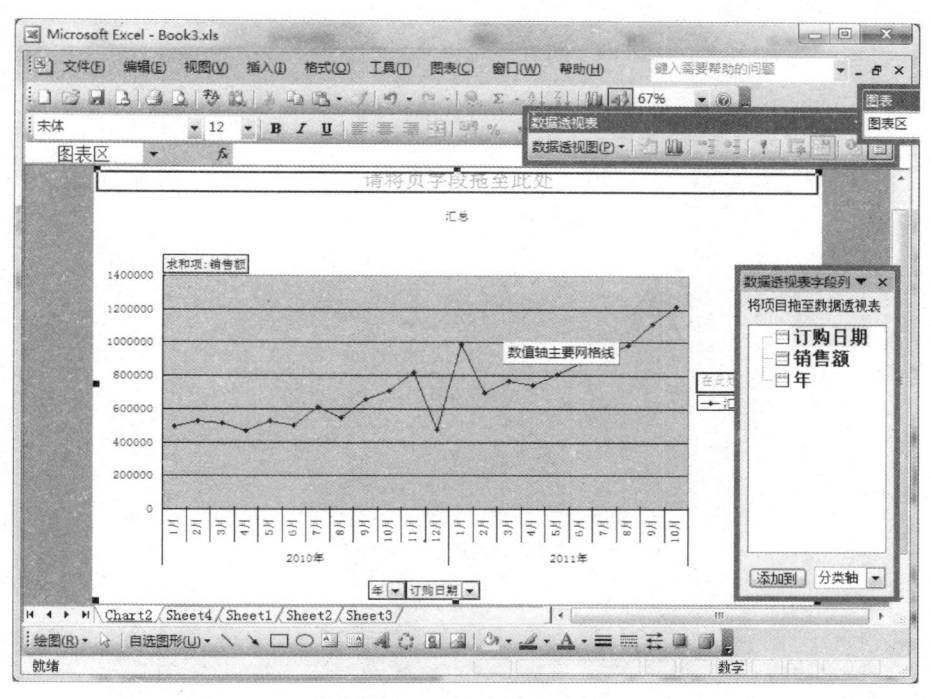

图 2.2.26　折线形数据透视图

步骤 3：添加趋势线，预测下月的销售情况。

通过对数据的观察，我们可以发现，各月的销售数据大体上满足随时间推移线性增长的规律。因此，可以采用线性模型描述变化规律。对准数据系列（蓝色的点）右击鼠标，选择"添加趋势线"→"类型"，选中"线性(L)"，如图 2.2.27 所示。选择"选项"，选定趋势线名称为"自动设置(A)：线性(汇总)"，选定趋势预测的"前推(F)"为"1"个周期，选中"显示公示(E)"和"显示 R 平方值(R)"，如图 2.2.28 所示。单击"确定"按钮，得到数据透视图，如图 2.2.29 所示。

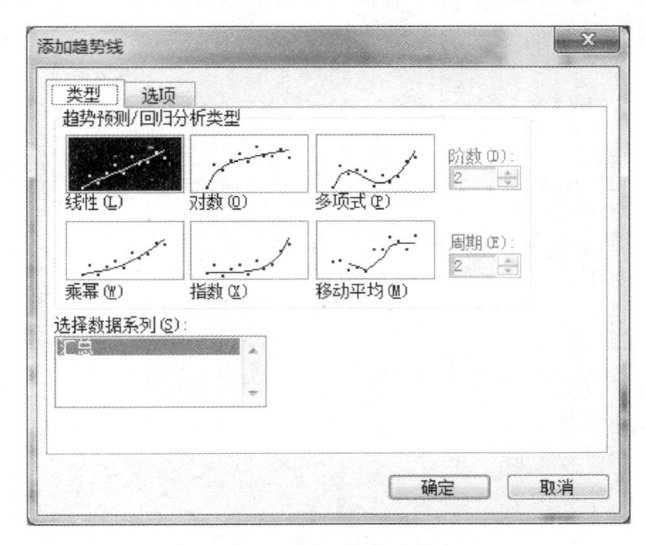

图 2.2.27　添加趋势线的类型

图 2.2.28 设定趋势线的选项

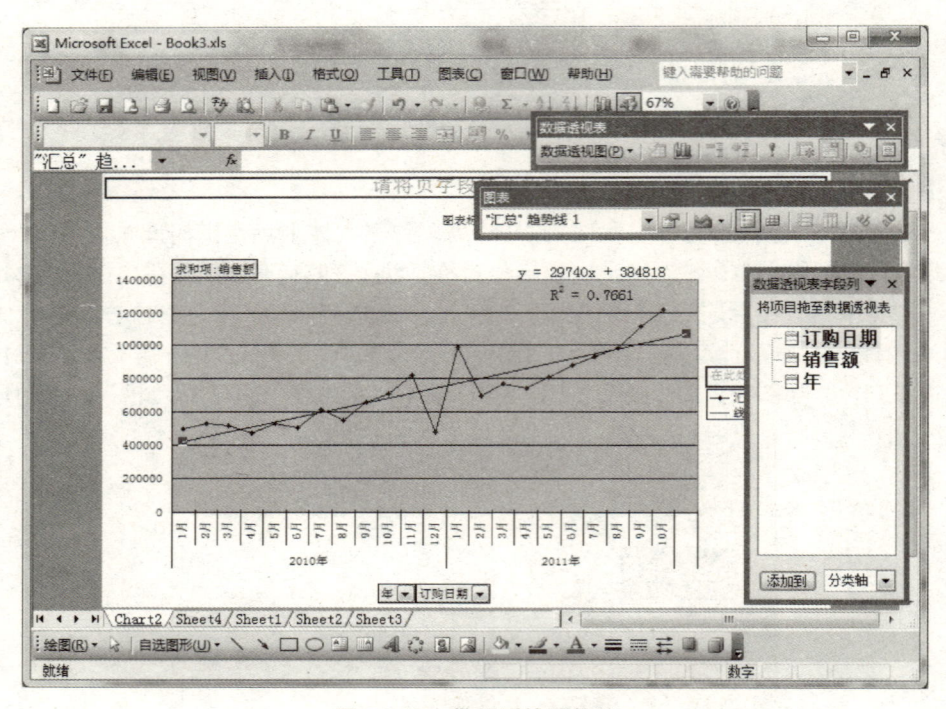

图 2.2.29 带预测的趋势线

观察如图 2.2.29 所示的数据透视图,可以发现该趋势线的方程为 $y=29\,740x+384\,818$,R^2 为 0.766 1(该统计量描述了回归分析拟合的好坏,超过 0.7 说明拟合得较好)。同时,可以观察到下个月的销售额约为 1 060 000 元。

集成实验指导3：网上商城的前后台功能体验

1. 前台操作

（1）充值

注册→登录→账户管理→充值。充值密码为登录密码。

（2）购买

注册→登录→查看商品→点击"购买"→到购物车中查看→购物车结账。结账密码为登录密码。

2. 后台操作

（1）登录

管理员是 Admin，密码是 Admin。

（2）添加商品

库存管理→添加商品→填写商品信息。

集成实验指导4：走近系统分析设计文档

1. 系统开发生命周期法（SDLC法）及其文档

系统开发生命周期（Systems Development Lifecycle，SDLC）是系统分析员、软件工程师、程序员以及最终用户建立计算机系统的一个过程，IBM称之为计算机应用开发周期。

系统开发生命周期包括以下六个阶段：

(1) 问题的定义及规划

系统规划主要是由系统分析员和用户讨论、了解情况，确定是否真的有必要建立一个新的计算机系统来取代原有的系统。

这一阶段的主要工作包括：企业目标的确定，解决目标的方式的确定，信息系统目标的确定，信息系统主要结构的确定，工程项目的确定，可行性研究等。

该阶段要求分析员如实地分析企业中发生的事情，然后，分析员与其他组织成员一起找出问题所在，这是项目其余阶段取得成功的关键。此阶段完成后要形成可行性分析报告和项目计划书。在项目的可行性分析中要进行技术可行性分析、经济可行性分析、执行可行性分析。一旦完成对每项可选实施方案的技术、经济和执行可行性的评估，就应该从中选择一种实施方案。可行性研究的目标是，对比各项可选实施方案，并提出一个最佳的实施方案。此外还要定义潜在的风险，特别是那些与项目的技术和执行可行性相关的潜在风险。关键的一点是应该将它们纳入风险评估文件，以便在项目实施过程中能够妥善处理它们。

(2) 需求分析

在确定软件开发可行的情况下，对软件需要实现的各个功能进行详细分析。需求分析阶段是一个很重要的阶段，这一阶段做得好，将为整个软件开发项目的成功打下良好的基础。"唯一不变的是变化本身。"同样，需求也是在整个软件开发过程中不断变化和深入的，因此我们必须制订需求变更计划来应付这种变化，以保护整个项目顺利进行。

此阶段要完成的工作包括：功能需求、性能需求、可靠性和可用性需求、出错处理需求、接口需求、约束、逆向需求，以及将来可能提出的要求的调查。最终要形成软件需求规格书。软件工程师首先必须与信息系统的使用者进行访谈，以辨认、了解目前的作业流程以及分辨哪些信息需求是必要的。这些初步的工作通常会记录在信息系统概念文件中，由信息系统的使用者自行准备或是由使用者与软件工程师共同来完成。因此，此阶段的工作环境与其他阶段不同，是到使用者所在地进行拜访。

(3) 系统设计

此阶段主要根据需求分析的结果，对整个软件系统进行设计，如系统框架设计、数据库设计等。系统设计一般分为总体设计和详细设计。好的系统设计将为软件程序编写打下良好的基础。

此阶段的主要工作包括：选定技术平台，设定项目目标，说明数据库要求，确定系统流程图，确定程序流程图，文件设计，描述所有输入/输出的格式和内容，完成详细的系统设计。这一阶段的最后一步工作是准备程序说明，其中包括各种程序模块的说明书。形成的文档包括功能说明书、软件非功能方面的技术指标描述、技术实现等。

(4) 程序编码

在这一阶段,分析员与程序员一起开发全部原始软件。此阶段要完成的工作是将软件设计的结果转换成计算机可运行的程序代码。在程序编码时必须制定统一的、符合标准的编写规范,以保证程序的可读性、易维护性,从而提高程序的运行效率。

(5) 系统测试

在这一阶段,程序员开始对系统及其文档进行测试和维护,以使系统运行更加稳健。在系统设计完成后要进行严密的测试,以发现系统在整个设计过程中存在的问题并加以纠正。整个测试过程分单元测试、组装测试以及系统测试三个阶段进行。测试的方法主要有白盒测试和黑盒测试两种。在测试过程中需要制订详细的测试计划并严格按照测试计划进行测试,以减少测试的随意性。形成的主要文档包括测试计划、测试用例、测试方案、系统测试报告、性能测试报告、用户操作手册等。测试并不是一个单一环节,而是贯穿于整个开发过程的。具体而言,从需求的描述开始,测试就应该开始了,但不是对代码的测试,而是制作测试用例,并且需要及时发现需求文档的问题,帮助分析人员在前期减少 BUG 存在的可能性。同理,设计过程中也离不开测试。

(6) 运行维护

系统维护是系统生命周期中持续时间最长的阶段。在系统开发完成并投入使用后,由于多方面的原因,系统不能继续适应用户的要求。要延续系统的使用寿命,就必须对系统进行维护。系统的维护包括纠错性维护和改进性维护两个方面。系统运行维护阶段要创建系统维护的方案、维护计划表、系统问题报告、系统修改报告等文档。

以上每个阶段都不是独立存在的,它们相互依存,构成系统开发的整个生命周期。

系统开发生命周期法(SDLC 法)的文档有两大特点:一是强调完备性和标准化,二是文档的编写工作量极大。

2. 系统需求分析文档

(1) 需求分析的任务和过程

需求分析的任务是借助当前系统的物理模型(待开发系统的系统元素)导出目标系统的逻辑模型(只描述系统要完成的功能和要处理的数据),解决目标系统"做什么"的问题,所要做的工作是深入描述软件的功能和性能,确定软件设计的限制和软件与其他系统元素的接口细节,定义软件的其他有效性需求,通过逐步细化对软件的要求来描述软件要处理的数据,并给软件开发提供一种可以转化为数据设计、结构设计和过程设计的数据与功能表示。必须全面理解用户的各项要求,但不能全盘接受,只能接受合理的要求;对其中模糊的要求要进一步澄清,然后决定是否采纳;对于无法实现的要求,要向用户做出充分的解释。最后将软件的需求准确地表达出来,形成软件需求说明书 SRS。

其实现步骤如下:

步骤 1:获得当前系统的物理模型。首先分析、理解当前系统是如何运行的,了解当前系统的组织机构、输入输出、资源利用情况和日常数据处理过程,并用一个具体的模型来反映对当前系统的理解。此步骤也可以称为"业务建模",其主要任务是对用户的组织机构或企业进行评估,理解其需要及未来系统要解决的问题,然后建立一个业务 USECASE 模型和业务对象模型。当然,如果系统相对简单,则没有必要大动干戈地进行业务建模,只要做一些简单的业务分析即可。

步骤 2:抽象出当前系统的逻辑模型。在理解当前系统"怎样做"的基础上,取出非本质因素,抽取出"做什么"的本质。

步骤 3:建立目标系统的逻辑模型——明确目标系统要"做什么"。

步骤 4:对逻辑模型进行补充,完善其他内容,如用户界面、启动和结束、出错处理、系统输入输出、系统性能、其他限制等。

需求分析的过程如下:

步骤 1:问题识别。即解决目标系统做什么,做到什么程度。需求包括:功能、性能、环境、可靠性、安全性、保密性、用户界面、资源使用、成本、进度。同时建立需求调查分析所需的通信途径。

步骤 2:分析与综合。即从数据流和数据结构出发,逐步细化所有的软件功能,找出各元素之间的联系、接口特性和设计上的限制,分析它们是否满足功能要求并剔除不合理部分,综合成系统解决方案,给出目标系统的详细逻辑模型。常用的分析方法包括面向数据流的结构化分析方法 SA(数据流图 DFD、数据词典 DD、加工逻辑说明),描绘系统数据关系的实体关系图 ERD,面向数据结构的 Jackson 方法 JSD,面向对象的分析方法 OOA(主要用 UML),对于有动态时序问题的软件可以用形式化技术,包括有穷状态机 FSM 的状态迁移(转换)图 STD、时序图、Petri 网或 Z 软件。每一种分析建模方法都有其优势和局限性,可以兼而有之,以不同的角度分析,避免陷入在软件需求方法和模型中发生教条的思维模式和派系斗争。一般来说,结构化方法用于中小规模软件,面向对象方法用于大型软件。

步骤 3:编制需求分析文档。

步骤 4:需求评审。

(2)文档规范

①编写方法

通常有三种编写方法:

一是用好的结构化和自然语言编写文本型文档。

二是建立图形化模型,用来描绘转换过程、系统状态,以及它们之间的变化、数据关系、逻辑流,或对象类与它们的关系。

三是编写形式化规格说明,这点可以通过使用数学上精确的形式化逻辑语言来定义需求。

多种编写方法可在同一个文档内使用,根据需要选择,或互为补充,以能够把需求说明白为目的。

②应有成果

a. 各业务手工办理流程文字说明;

b. 各业务手工办理流程图;

c. 各业务手工办理各环节输入输出表单、数据来源;

d. 目标软件系统功能划分(示意图及文字说明);

e. 目标软件系统中各业务办理流程文字说明;

f. 目标软件系统中各业务办理流程图(模型);

g. 目标软件系统中各业务办理各环节数据、数据采集方式、数据间的内在联系分析;

h. 目标软件系统用户界面图、各式系统逻辑模型图及说明。

③文档工具推荐

a. 调研结果"需求分析说明书"格式参照开发文档模板;

  b. 单位组织结构图、功能模块分解图用 VISIO 绘制,或直接用 Word 中的画图工具;

  c. 业务流程图用 VISIO 中的 FLOWCHART 模板绘制;

  d. 系统逻辑模型使用 ROSE 绘制或者用 VISIO 中的 UML 模板绘制;

  e. 软件用户界面用 VISIO 中的 WIN95 USER INTERFACE 模板绘制;

  f. 数据物理模型用 POWERDESINER 绘制。

④需求文档编写原则

  a. 句子简短完整,具有正确的语法、拼写和标点。

  b. 使用的术语与词汇表中所定义的一致。

  c. 需求陈述应该有一致的样式,例如,"系统必须……"或者"用户必须……",并紧跟一个行为动作和可观察的结果。

  d. 避免使用模糊、主观的术语,减少不确定性,如"界面友好、操作方便"。

  e. 避免使用比较性词语,如"提高",应定量说明提高程度。

3. 系统设计文档

(1)系统概要设计文档

系统概要设计使得项目组内成员对整个系统的主要功能及其概要的实现手段有一个宏观的把握,是整个系统最雏形同时也是最基本的引导性文档。概要设计有多种方法。在早期有模块化方法、功能分解方法;在 20 世纪 60 年代后期提出了面向数据流和面向数据结构的设计方法;近年来又提出面向对象的设计方法等。

系统概要设计文档样例如下:

```
1  引言
1.1 编写目的
1.2 背景
1.3 定义
1.4 参考资料

2  总体设计
2.1 需求规定
2.2 运行环境
2.3 基本设计概念和处理流程
2.4 结构
2.5 功能需求与程序的关系
2.6 人工处理过程
2.7 尚未解决的问题

3  接口
3.1 用户接口
3.2 外部接口
3.3 内部接口
```

续表

```
4  运行
4.1 运行模块组合
4.2 运行控制
4.3 运行时间

5  结构设计
5.1 逻辑结构设计要点
5.2 物理结构设计要点
5.3 数据结构与程序的关系

6  其他
6.1 出错信息
6.2 补救措施
6.3 系统维护设计
```

(2) 系统详细设计文档

详细设计说明书又称程序设计说明书,其编制目的是为了说明对一个软件系统各个层次中的每一个程序(每个模块或子程序)的设计考虑。如果一个软件系统比较简单,层次很少,则该文件可以不单独编写,有关内容可并入概要设计文档。

系统详细设计文档样例如下:

```
1. 引言
1.1 编写目的和范围
1.2 术语表
1.3 参考资料
1.4 使用的文字处理和绘图工具

2. 全局数据结构说明
2.1 常量
2.2 变量
2.3 数据结构

3. 模块设计
3.1 用例图
3.2 功能设计说明

4. 接口设计
4.1 内部接口
4.2 外部接口
4.2.1 接口说明
4.2.2 调用方式
```

续表

5. 数据库设计
6. 系统安全保密设计
6.1 说明
6.2 设计
6.2.1 数据传输部分
6.2.2 IP 过滤分部
6.2.3 身份验证部分
7. 系统性能设计
8. 系统出错处理

无论是面向过程还是对象,都要重视设计文档,但设计文档规范要么是需要与名字命名规范等有关编程的细节,要么就是利用已经编写好的程序想当然地抽象出相应的设计文档规范格式,或者从项目管理的要求出发,设计相应的文档格式等。这三种做法的后果就是利用规范无法指导设计工作的开展,编写的设计文档不可操作。事实上,从系统分析文档转换成相应的可以指导编程的设计文档是一种客观存在的思维活动,有其内在的规律,这种规律既对系统分析内容的采集和抽象以及描述提出了规范要求,又要求在系统分析描述时能自然过渡到软件设计,最终的结果就是能利用程序语言对现实世界的描述模式(主要分为两种:面向对象和面向过程)来描述系统分析。可见,程序语言的描述模式越接近现实世界,在从现实世界的模型转换成程序语言的模型时就越自然;在转换过程中采用的手段越符合其内在的规律,其输出的结果设计文档就越具有可控性。

② 集成实验报告

集成实验报告 1

实验项目名称　保证输入数据的正确性
实　验　室　　信息管理与工程学院机房
所属课程名称　信息系统导论
实　验　类　型　基础型
实　验　日　期　_____

班　　级　_____
学　　号　_____
姓　　名　_____
成　　绩　_____

实验概述：

【实验目的及要求】
目的：
1. 了解降低数据出错概率的方法；
2. 为学习"数据结构""数据库"课程打基础。
要求：
1. 学习 Access 中的"输入掩码"知识点；
2. 学习 Access 中的"下拉菜单"知识点。

【实验原理】
1. 通过使用"输入掩码"技术控制录入数据的类型和位数；
2. 通过制定"下拉菜单"避免超范围的录入；
3. 通过增加数据录入的自动化程度，即利用数据导入，减少错误。

【实验环境】（使用的软、硬件）
1. Windows XP；
2. Microsoft Access 2003 及以上版本；
3. Microsoft Excel 2003 及以上版本；
4. 台式机或笔记本。

实验内容：

1. 在 Microsoft Access 数据库中建立网上商城"产品类别表"，要求：
(1)表中含有三列，分别是类别 ID、类别名称、典型图片；
(2)类别 ID 构成是 1 位数字加下划线加三个字母形式，如"1_ABC"；
(3) 类别名称只限于"手机导航仪、电脑设备、办公设备、数码产品、电视家庭影音、厨卫器具"六种；
(4)图片是对象连接与嵌入类型。
结果截图：
(1)类别 ID 输入掩码成功证据：

(2)类别名称下拉菜单成功证据：

(3)建好的空表显示：

(4)录入两条自编正确的数据，显示证据：

(5)录入一条错误的数据，显示报错提示：

续表

2. 将"网上商城系统数据库"中的数据表 tb_Class 导入 Access 数据库,表名不变,显示证据截图:

备注或简要说明(如需要)

【小结】(心得体会、思考和建议)

指导教师评语及成绩:

成绩: 指导教师签名:

批阅日期:

集成实验报告 2

实验项目名称　<u>网上商城的销售决策分析</u>
实　验　室　　<u>信息管理与工程学院机房</u>
所属课程名称　<u>信息系统导论</u>
实　验　类　型　<u>基础型</u>
实　验　日　期　<u>　　　　　　　　　　　　</u>

班　　　级　<u>　　　　　　　　　　　　</u>
学　　　号　<u>　　　　　　　　　　　　</u>
姓　　　名　<u>　　　　　　　　　　　　</u>
成　　　绩　<u>　　　　　　　　　　　　</u>

实验概述：

【实验目的及要求】
目的：
1. 了解从数据库查询数据、数据汇总以及预测决策的方法；
2. 掌握利用 Microsoft Query 进行数据查询的步骤；
3. 掌握利用 Microsoft Excel 进行数据分类汇总的步骤；
4. 掌握利用 Microsoft Excel 进行销售预测决策分析的步骤。

要求：
利用 Microsoft Office，查询汇总销售数据，并预测未来的销售情况。

【实验原理】
1. 通过 Office 软件，获取企业数据中保存的详细数据，从而帮助企业了解生产经营具体情况；
2. 通过 Office 软件，对数据加以汇总并预测，从而帮助企业了解未来发展的趋势。

【实验环境】（使用的软、硬件）
1. Windows XP；
2. Microsoft Access 2003 及以上版本；
3. Microsoft Excel 2003 及以上版本；
4. 台式机或笔记本。

实验内容：

1. 网上商城的数据已经导入"网上商城系统数据库数据.xls"文件中，请采用合适的方法，查询 2010 年 1 月～2011 年 10 月的销售数据，将这些数据按照月份进行汇总，并且利用汇总结果，预测未来一个月——2011 年 11 月的销售情况。
结果截图：
(1) 建立 ODBC 数据源的截图：

(2) 查询 2010 年 1 月～2011 年 10 月销售数据的截图：

(3) 制作数据透视表按月汇总销售数据的截图：

(4) 绘制数据透视图预测未来销售额的截图：

备注或简要说明（如需要）

2 集成实验报告

【小结】(心得体会、思考和建议)

指导教师评语及成绩：

成绩：

指导教师签名：
批阅日期：

集成实验报告 3

实验项目名称　　网上商城的前后台功能体验
实　验　室　　　信息管理与工程学院机房
所属课程名称　　信息系统导论
实　验　类　型　　基础型
实　验　日　期　　_____

班　　　级　_____
学　　　号　_____
姓　　　名　_____
成　　　绩　_____

2 集成实验报告

实验概述：

【实验目的及要求】
目的：
1. 体验网上商城的前后台功能,体会 B2C 商务模式和特点；
2. 为后续的电子商务、程序设计、Web 开发等课程打下基础。
要求：
1. 了解网上商城前台的购物流程和充值流程；
2. 了解网上商城后台的管理。

【实验原理】
　　通过操作基于实验平台的网上商城,使学生对网上商城的架构和功能有进一步的了解,尤其是后台管理和支付充值这一块内容的深入,是非模拟网上应用系统不能提供的,在体验式了解的基础上,实现本门课程理论与实践的结合,并为后续课程做好铺垫。

【实验环境】(使用的软、硬件)
1. Windows XP；
2. IE、Firefox 等浏览器；
3. 台式机或笔记本；
4. 具备上网条件。

实验内容：

1. 前台操作
连接网上商城 http://202.121.143.200:801/。
(1)注册一个用户,显示证据截图：

(2)完成一个商品的购买流程,总结购买流程,显示结账截图：

(3)进行虚拟充值,显示证据截图：

2. 后台操作
注：后台网址请点击前台网页最下面的后台管理。
　　管理员是 Admin,密码是 Admin。
(1)添加一个新的管理员,显示证据截图：

(2)添加 2 件商品,显示证据截图：

3. 结合知名网站亚马逊,分析该网站的优缺点,给出提升其功能的建议。

备注或简要说明(如需要)

【小结】（心得体会、思考和建议）

指导教师评语及成绩：

成绩：

指导教师签名：
批阅日期：

集成实验报告 4

实验项目名称　　走近系统分析设计文档
实　验　室　　信息管理与工程学院机房
所属课程名称　　信息系统导论
实　验　类　型　　基础型
实　验　日　期　　

班　　　级　　
学　　　号　　
姓　　　名　　
成　　　绩

实验概述：

【实验目的及要求】

目的：

1. 更好地了解系统开发生命周期法(SDLC 法)，尤其是其文档的特点和作用；
2. 体验系统分析文档与系统设计文档的重要性，以及相互关系；
3. 体会系统分析与设计对系统实现的重要影响；
4. 为学习"系统分析和设计"课程打基础。

要求：

1. 阅读基于实验平台的网上商城系统分析、设计文档；
2. 结合以上实验目的做相关分析。

【实验原理】

　　掌握系统开发生命周期法(SDLC 法)中关于需求分析、系统设计(概要设计和详细设计)等阶段的内容。掌握 SDLC 法中关于系统开发文档的特点和作用。

【实验环境】(使用的软硬件)

1. Windows XP；
2. Microsoft Word 2003 及以上版本；
3. Microsoft Excel 2003 及以上版本；
4. Visio 或 Power Designer；
5. 台式机或笔记本。

实验内容：

在相关文档阅读的基础上，分别回答如下问题：

1. 系统开发生命周期法(SDLC 法)的文档有什么特点和作用？

2. 系统分析文档如何转化为系统设计文档？

3. 探讨系统分析与设计对系统实现的影响。

4. 评价该网上商城文档的优劣之处，并指出需要提高的地方。

备注或简要说明(如需要)

2　集成实验报告

【小结】（心得体会、思考和建议）

指导教师评语及成绩：

成绩：

指导教师签名：
批阅日期：

参考文献

[1] Stephen Haag, Maeve Cummings: *Management Information Systems for the Information Age* (9th Edition)(《信息时代的管理信息系统》,英文版·原书第9版),机械工业出版社2017年版。

[2] Kenneth C. Laudon, Jane P. Laudon:《管理信息系统:管理数字化公司》(第11版),清华大学出版社2011年版。

[3] (美)肯尼思·劳东(Kenneth C. Laudon)、简·劳东(Jane P. Laudon)著,劳帼龄译:《管理信息系统》(第13版),中国人民大学出版社2016年版。

[4] (美)戴维·M.克伦克(David M. Kroenke)著,贾素玲等译:《管理信息系统》(原书第6版),机械工业出版社2014年版。

[5] 腾佳东主编:《管理信息系统实验》(第2版),东北财经大学出版社2013年版。

[6] 李静编著:《管理信息系统实验教程》,北京师范大学出版社2011年版。

[7] 王晓燕主编:《管理信息系统实验》,经济科学出版社2010年版。

[8] 涂智寿主编:《管理信息系统实验》,西南财经大学出版社2012年版。